CW01480917

Passport to
IELTS

Diana Hopkins

Mark Nettle

MACMILLAN PUBLISHERS

INTRODUCTION

▶ To the student

What is this book for?

This book is designed to help you if you are planning to take the IELTS test. The IELTS test consists of four sections: a reading test, a writing test, a listening test from a cassette, and an interview. Each unit of this book gives you practice for each section of the test, as well as targeting specific skills that will help you, both in the test and in your use of English generally.

How to use this book

There are ten units in the book. The first part of each unit is a reading, writing, listening and speaking test paper. After the test paper there is a key containing answers and notes. At the end of each unit there are one or two SKILLS FOCUS sections. You will find tapescripts for all recorded material at the back of the book.

It is important that you try to do the reading and writing tests within the time limit suggested. This will give you realistic practice in working under time pressure. The IELTS listening cassette is played only once so you should only play your cassette once, too. Of course, you may wish to listen to the recording a second time *after* you have checked your answers.

Many of the speaking practice sections work best if you have a partner, although if you cannot find a partner it is useful to study the sections anyway.

When you have completed the test part of the unit you should check your answers using the key. Then work through each SKILLS FOCUS at your own pace.

The units become progressively closer to a full-length IELTS test, so you should do them in order. However, you may wish to refer to a particular SKILLS FOCUS at any time or work through it more than once.

Unit 10 is a complete practice IELTS test. You should do it under test conditions if possible. If you are working without a teacher you will not be able to do the interview part of the test. When you have completed the full test, following the instructions carefully, you should check your answers and then look at the score guide.

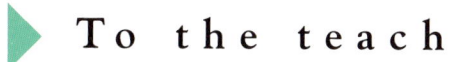

To the teacher

This book has been designed with either class use or self-study in mind. Obviously, you need to familiarise yourself with the IELTS test (specimen materials are available from IELTS centres). Before using the book it would also be helpful if the students were made aware of the structure of the test.

We suggest that you do the test paper part of each unit (see *To the student*) under timed test conditions, following each section with a group discussion of the answers and any difficulties. We have found that the practice papers help to build students' confidence and ability to deal with unfamiliar question types under timed conditions. However, special attention should also be paid to the SKILLS FOCUS sections which provide an opportunity to practise and improve sub-skills demanded by the test. We suggest that these sections should be worked on in pairs or groups.

The maze in Unit 8 is more fun if you cut up the cards beforehand and only issue a group with a card as they require it. The test paper in Unit 10 includes an interview in the speaking section. While you are carrying out the interviews in a separate room, the remaining students could be using the SKILLS FOCUS sections for revision. The interview needs to be as authentic as possible; an elicitation task should be devised along the lines of those in Units 5, 6, and 7, or one of these could be used again. If you do not have access to the IELTS speaking test band descriptors, you should give your students generalised feedback on their interviews similar to that given in the score guide.

CONTENTS

UNIT	TOPIC	PRACTICE PAPER				KEY	SKILLS FOCUS
1 Pages 7-17	**ARRIVING IN BRITAIN**	Reading: short extracts	Writing: Task: a letter	Listening: 1 task: choosing a picture	Speaking: exchanging personal information	Key and feedback	• Understanding intructions • Talking about yourself
2 Pages 18-30	**WATER**	Reading: 1 passage	Writing: Task: describing statistics	Listening: 1 task: filling a form	Speaking: asking questions – a job interview	Key and feedback	• Scan reading • Writing: describing tables and charts
3 Pages 31-39	**ANIMALS**	Reading: 1 passage	Writing: Task: argument/ opinion	Listening: 1 task: T/F/NM	Speaking: about your customs and culture	Key and feedback	• Speaking: a topic in detail • Listening for gist
4 Pages 40-50	**TECHNOLOGY**	Reading: 1 passage	Writing: Task: describing how something works	Listening: 1 task: a summary	Speaking: explaining and describing	Key and feedback	• Skim reading • Writing: desribing how something works
5 Pages 51-62	**RECYCLING**	Reading: 2 passages	Writing: Task: describing a process	Listening: 1 task: open questions	Speaking: eliciting information 1	Key and feedback	• Asking questions • Listening for specific information

UNIT	TOPIC	PRACTICE PAPER			KEY	SKILLS FOCUS
6 Pages 63-76	LIVING IN BRITAIN	Reading: 2 passages	Writing: Task: a letter	Listening: 2 tasks: pictures, form filling	Speaking: eliciting Information 2	Key and feedback	• Writing a letter seeking information • Reading: gap-filling tasks
7 Pages 77-90	HEALTH	Reading: 2 passages	Writing: Task: expanding skeleton notes	Listening: 2 tasks: true/false, summary	Speaking: eliciting Information 3	Key and feedback	• Reading: guessing meaning from context • Speaking: intonation in questions
8 Pages 91-108	EDUCATION	Reading: 2 passages	Writing: Task: an essay	Listening: 2 tasks: filling a table, open questions	Speaking: an IELTS maze	Key and feedback	• Writing an argument
9 Pages 109-122	GLOBAL WARMING	Reading: 3 passages	Writing: Task: an essay	Listening: 3 tasks: filling a table, open questions, summary	Speaking: speculating	Key and feedback	• Speaking: speculating about the future
10 Pages 123-137	SAFETY	Reading: 3 passages	Writing: Task: describing statistics Task: an essay	Listening: 30 minutes	Speaking: the IELTS Interview	Key, feedback and score guide	

5

First published 1993
Reprinted 1994

Published by MACMILLAN PUBLISHERS LTD

London and Basingstoke

ISBN 0-333-58706-5

Illustrations by Jane Cheswright
Produced by **AMR**
Printed in Malaysia

A catalogue record for this book is available from the British Library

Acknowledgements
The authors and publishers would particularly like to thank the following for permission to reproduce copyright material. We should be pleased to hear from any copyright holder we have been unable to contact.

Unit 1   Arriving in the UK

Reading:
Extract 1 *British Airways High Life*, 8/92
Extract 2 *London Shopping Guide*, Tailor Made Media 1992
Extract 3 *How to call home from the UK*, British Telecom 1992
Extract 4 *Visitors' Guide*, B A A Heathrow

Unit 2   Water

Reading: *New Internationalist*, May 1990
Writing: *New Internationalist*, May 1990
Skills Focus: Scan
Reading 1 *Education Guardian*, 8 Jan 1991
2 *New Internationalist*, May 1990
Writing 1 *Education Guardian*, 8 Jan 1991
2 *New Internationalist*, Feb 1990

Unit 3   Animals

Reading: *BBC Wildlife Magazine*, March 1991

Unit 4   Technology

Reading: *New Civil Engineer*, May 1991 (adapted)
Listening: *New Scientist*, 31 Aug 1991

Unit 5   Recycling

Reading: *New Scientist*, 8 Sept 1990
Writing: *New Scientist*, 19 Oct 1991

Unit 6   Living in the UK

Reading Passage 1: Muiwzer, G, *New to the UK*, Routledge & Kegan Paul London/New York
Reading Passage 2: *New Internationalist*, July 1990
Skills Focus: Practice 2: *The Guardian*, 4 July 1991
Practice 3: *New Statesman & Society*, June 1988

Unit 7   Health

Reading: *New Scientist*, 3 Nov 1990

Unit 8   Education

Reading Passage 1: Bishop, G, *Alternative strategies for Education*, Macmillan, 1989
Reading Passage 2: *Times Educational Supplement*, May 3 1991

Unit 9   Global Warming

Reading Passages 1 and 2: *New Internationalist*, April 1990
Reading Passage 3: *Newsweek*, 22 April 1991
Listening Section 3: (*Education Guardian*), 8 *January 1991*

Unit 10   Safety:

Reading Passages 1 and 2: *New Scientist*, 4 Jan 1992
Reading Passage 3: *Sunday Times Magazine*, 20 August 1989

UNIT 1 ARRIVING IN BRITAIN

▶ **R e a d i n g** *You should spend no more than 15 minutes on questions 1-10.*

Questions 1-3 refer to **Extract 1**, *Arriving at London airports*

Decide if the following statements are TRUE, FALSE, or if the information you need is not given according to **Extract 1**, and write T for true, F for false, or NG for not given in the space provided. The first one has been done for you as an example.

Example: If you want to visit London you should follow the ARRIVALS sign.   T

1 If you want to transfer to an international flight, you should follow the transfer sign.   ——

2 You can collect your baggage from any carousel.   ——

3 When you reach the Arrivals Hall you have completed airport formalities.   ——

Extract 1   Arriving at London airports

- Just follow these simple steps for a trouble-free arrival.

- Follow the ARRIVALS sign if you are ending your journey in London or transferring to a UK domestic flight.

- This will take you to the Immigration Hall where you must present your passport and any necessary visa/health documentation.

- At HEATHROW airport proceed downstairs to claim your baggage from the carousel indicating your flight number. At GATWICK airport proceed downstairs in the North Terminal to claim your baggage from the carousel indicating your flight number. Free trolleys are available for your bags.

- To clear customs take the Red Channel if you have goods to declare or the Green Channel if you have no goods to declare.

- You will then be in the Arrivals Hall. From here you can obtain transport into central London; transfer between Gatwick and Heathrow airports and transfer to UK domestic flights.

Question 4 refers to **Extract 2** *below.*

Extract 2

Thomas Cook
Foreign Exchange

- Instant availability of travellers cheques and major currencies.
- Extended opening hours and open on Saturdays too.
- Thomas Cook travellers' cheques encashed free of charge.

Foreign Exchange isn't foreign to us.

4 Choose the best letter **A, B, C** or **D** and write it in the space provided. **Extract 2** is an advertisement for:

    A a travel agent
    B a restaurant
    C a money changer
    D a souvenir shop

Your answer _____

5 *Question 5 refers to* **Extract 3**. In the box below are instructions for using a phonecard in a payphone in Britain. Match each instruction **(i - v)** with its corresponding picture **(A - E)**, and write the letter of the picture in the space provided. The first one has been done for you as an example.

Extract 3   Using a phonecard

i	Lift receiver, check dialling tone.	**Example:** ___E___
ii	Insert phonecard, green side up.	____
iii	Dial number and wait for connection.	____
iv	When call is finished replace receiver.	____
v	Your phonecard will be ejected.	____

    A   B   C   D   E

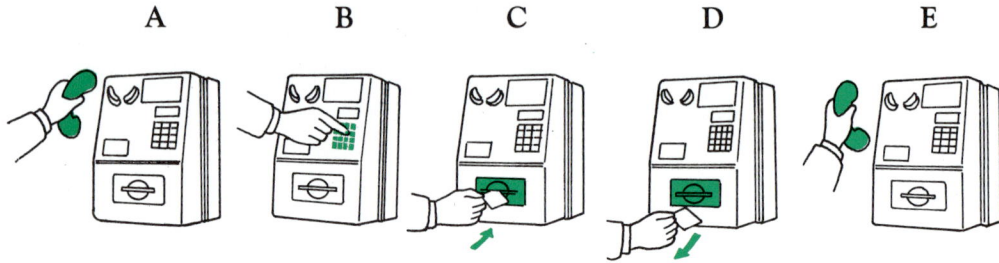

Questions 6-10 refer to **Extract 4, Getting into London from the airport,** *below.*

Extract 4   Getting into London from the airport

TAXI
You will have no difficulty finding one of the famous black taxis to take you to central London. The metered fare to Oxford Street will be in the region of £30 dependent on traffic. The taxis carry up to 5 passengers and the driver will not charge more than is shown on the meter. You may tip the driver (most Londoners do) but you don't have to.

UNDERGROUND
In London the underground is called 'The Tube' and is a cheap and efficient way to travel. Heathrow has two underground stations, clearly signposted from the terminals, on the Piccadilly Line, which runs directly into the heart of the city. Heathrow is on a loop in the line so it is impossible to get on a train going in the wrong direction. It will take about 50 minutes to get to central London and the adult single fare is £2.50. Special Travelcards are also available offering unlimited travel on public transport. You can purchase your tickets at the entrance to the station.

BY BUS
'Airbuses' run from the central bus station and are a great way to see London from the comfort of a coach as you are driven into the city. The cost of a single journey is £5. If you're at Terminal 4 take a free transfer bus to the station. If you are heading into central London at night you can catch the N97 bus from the central bus station which costs £2.00.

Answer these questions by writing a word or short phrase in the space provided.

6   What does the cost of a taxi from the airport to London depend on?

_____

7   How do you know how much to pay for a taxi?

_____

8   Why is it impossible to get on a tube train at Heathrow going in the wrong direction?

_____

9   What kind of ticket allows you to travel on a bus or an underground train?

_____

10   What are two advantages of travelling by coach to London?

_____

W r i t i n g *You should spend no more than 15 minutes on this task.*

Next month you are coming to Britain to study at a university in Scotland. On the way you have a two-day stopover in London. You need accommodation for one night and you would like to use this time to see as much as possible of London. As a student you have a limited budget.

 **Write a letter to the London Travel Information Centre explaining your situation and asking for advice on accommodation and sight-seeing.**

You do *not* need to write addresses. You should write at least 80 words.

Begin:

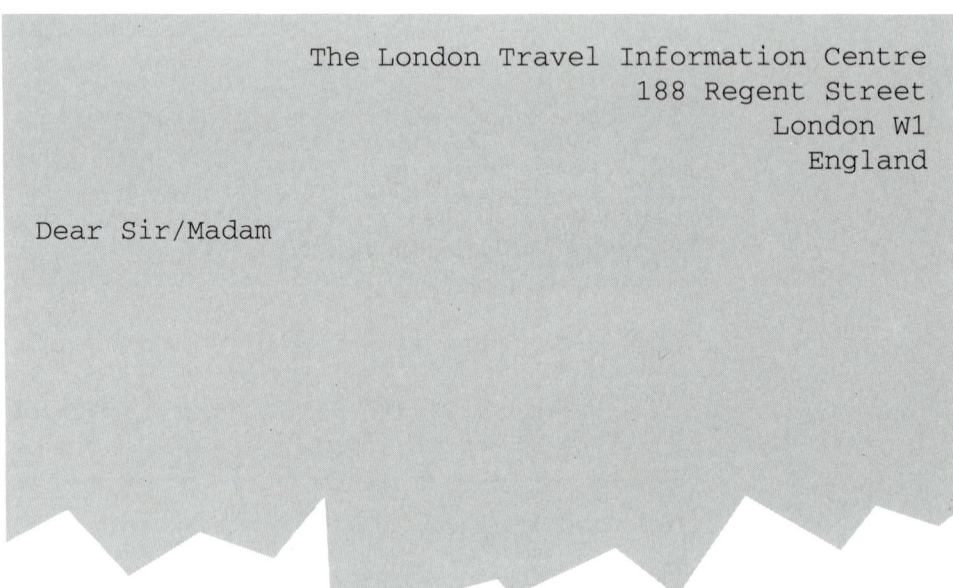

```
                        The London Travel Information Centre
                                    188 Regent Street
                                         London W1
                                           England


Dear Sir/Madam
```

Listening

As you listen to the tape, decide which of the pictures best fits what you hear and circle the letter beside that picture. We have done the first one for you.

Example: How did Bill find his way to the Hall of Residence?

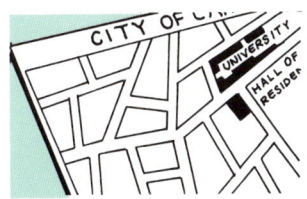

A

B

(C)

D

1 How did Bill travel from London to Newcastle?

A

B

C

D

2 What does Bill look like now?

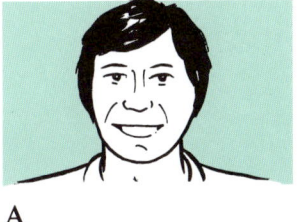

A

B

C

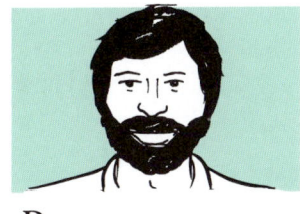

D

3 Which room is Bill's room?

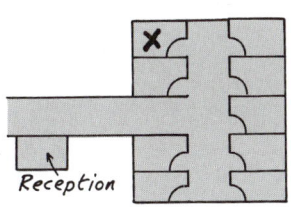

A

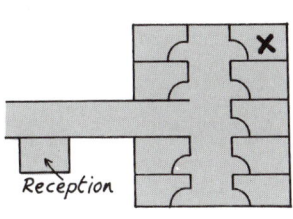

B

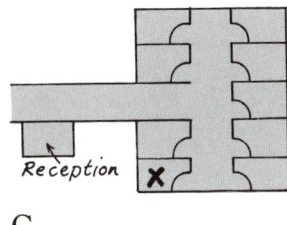

C

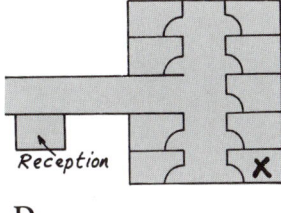

D

4 What time is the meeting for new students?

A

B

C

D

Speaking

The following personal information questions could all be answered by simply saying 'yes' or 'no' or by using a single word. However, in an interview situation you will give a much better impression by answering them as fully as possible.

Look at the first question below and a possible answer, and then answer the remaining questions by giving as much information about yourself as possible.

Example question: Are you married?
Example answer: Yes, I am. My husband's a teacher at a local college.

1 Have you got any children?

2 What do you do exactly?

3 Where are you from?

4 How long have you lived here/there?

5 What do you like doing in your spare time?

6 Have you ever been abroad?

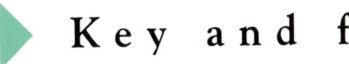

Key and feedback

Reading

EXTRACT 1
1   NG
2   F
3   T

EXTRACT 2
4   C

EXTRACT 3
5 ii C   iv   A
   iii B   v   D

EXTRACT 4
6   traffic
7   it is shown on the meter
     (or similar)
8   there's a loop
9   Travelcards
10   you can see London / comfort

Did you understand the instructions?
See the SKILLS FOCUS in this unit-
Understanding Instructions, page 15.

You need to take care with this type
of question; all four are needed for one
point.

Notice you only had to write 'a word
or short phrase' – not a sentence.

Both for one point again.

Writing

Was your letter relevant to the question? Did you **(i)** explain your situation, **(ii)**
ask about accommodation and **(iii)** ask about sightseeing? You could have used
some of the following phrases:

I am coming to Britain next month.

I will have two days in London before travelling to Scotland.

I would be grateful if you could send me some information about…

As a student my budget is limited.

Did you leave yourself enough time to check your work within the 15 minutes?
When you write you should always check your work, and the box on the next
page gives guidelines for checking which you may wish to refer to when you do
any of the writing tasks in this book, or *any* writing in English.

Writing: things you can check yourself

- *Relevance:*   Have you answered the question set?

- *Agreement:*   Do your verbs agree with their subjects?
  Example: A good teacher listens to students.
  Good students listen to their teacher.

- *Plurals:*   We use plurals without an article to speak generally.
  Example: Ants are social insects.

- *Articles:*   (*a, an, the*) Check that singular countable nouns have an article in front of them.

- *Tense:*   Look at each verb and ask yourself which tense you have used, and why you used it.

Listening

1	B	3	D
2	A	4	D

Did you spend time studying the pictures before you listened? This helps greatly as you have so little time *while* you listen.

Speaking

Did you manage to give full answers? See the SKILLS FOCUS in this unit - *Talking about Yourself*, page 17.

Skills Focus
Understanding instructions

In this unit you had to deal with these instructions:

…write T for true, F for false, or NG for not given…

Choose the best letter A, B, C or D and write it in the space provided.

Match each instruction (i- v) with its corresponding picture (A-E)…

Answer each question by writing a word or short phrase…

…circle the letter beside that picture.

Did you find these instructions easy to follow? Did you follow them exactly? It is very important to follow instructions accurately in your IELTS test; you should spend time reading instructions as well as questions.

Practice I

What's wrong with the way this candidate has answered the following questions?

1 Choose the best alternative, **A, B, C** or **D** and write the letter in the space provided.

The capital of Britain is:

A Edinburgh
B London   **Your answer**
C Manchester
D Cardiff   _London_

2 Decide if the following statement is true or false, and write **A** if it is true or **B** if it is false, in the space provided.

Heathrow is Britain's largest airport.   _T_

3 Complete the following sentence using *one* or *two* words.

The number of tourists visiting Britain _is going up_ every year.

4 Answer the following question using a short phrase.

How can you make a collect (reverse charge) call from a British payphone?

You can make a collect call by dialling 155 or the home country
direct number.

Practice 2

Follow these instructions carefully!

1 Choose the adjective which best describes how you feel now, and circle the appropriate letter.

A happy
B sad
C bored
D interested
E frustrated

2 Use *one* or *two* words to complete the following sentence.

The IELTS is a _____ test.

3 Read the following passage, and then complete the summary below using one word, *taken from the passage*, to fill each gap.

Passage

One IELTS candidate had a very unfortunate experience because he did not follow the instructions he was given. During the reading part of the test he wrote all his answers on the question booklet instead of his answer sheet. He scored a band 1.

Summary

Due to _____ following _____ , one IELTS candidate _____ a band 1.

Skills Focus
Talking about yourself

In the speaking section of this unit you had to answer questions about yourself. 'Personal information' questions in your IELTS interview could ask about your:

job
interests
family
study
home town
ambitions

As we suggested, it is important to provide full answers rather than single words; remember the examiner wants to know about *your* spoken English ability, not his or her *own* ability! The examiner will encourage this by asking questions such as, *Can you tell me about your family?* (an 'open' question) rather than *Have you got any children?* (a 'yes/no' question).

Practice 1

Which of the *answers* to the questions below do you think are good answers? Why (not)?

Question	Answer
Where do you live?	In São Paulo.
Where are you from?	Well, I was born in Beijing, but I've lived in Shanghai since I was 4.
What do you like doing in your spare time?	I like football and cricket.
Can you tell me about your research?	Yes, I'm part of a team at the university trying to develop a low-cost satellite communication system for Third World countries.

Practice 2

Read the dialogue below.

Interviewer:	Right, so tell me about your family.
Candidate:	Well, I have two children, two boys and a girl. My wife's a nurse and all of my children are at primary school.
Interviewer:	Oh, I see. And do you live in the capital of your country?
Candidate:	Yes, we do. We've got a small flat – too small really, but we're used to it. We share a garden with other residents in the block.

Now ask a partner to ask you the same questions asked in the dialogue, and a few more using the 'Personal Information' topics at the top of the page.

> ### Reading *You should spend no more than 25 minutes on questions 1-18.*

Questions 1-3

Answer these questions using the reading passage, **The grand embankment**. The first one has been done as an example.

Your answers

Example: Who is the World Bank Vice-President
for Asia?   <u>Atilla Karaosmanoglu</u>

1 What is the population of Bangladesh?   _____

2 Who proposed a $10 000 million scheme?   _____

3 What was revealed in London in 1989?   _____

Questions 4-7

The reading passage, **The grand embankment**, describes a situation, a problem, a proposed solution to the problem, the implementation of the proposal, and includes a disadvantage and various criticisms of the proposal. Match the labels (**4-7**) with the sentences in the box opposite. Note that there are more sentences than you need. Write only one letter in each space.

The first one has been done as an example.

The grand embankment

Situation: The yearly monsoon leads to rising waters in Bangladesh.

Your answers

Example: The problem   <u>C</u>

4 A proposed solution   _____

5 A disadvantage of the proposal   _____

6 The implementation of the proposal   _____

7 One criticism of the proposal   _____

Conclusion: Care should be taken in implementing the proposal.

A The World Bank Action Plan
B Computerised flood control systems
C Flooding can be disastrous
D Disagreement amongst investors
E Embankments along all the major rivers
F Land would be taken from people
G High cost which could lead to debt
H No-one knows more about managing the flood waters than the Bangladeshis

The grand embankment

Bangladesh's floods can be devastating. But an ambitious scheme to control the waters is also causing concern.

1 No country is as profoundly influenced by water as Bangladesh. The land, culture and lifestyles of the people are shaped by three of the world's most powerful rivers – the Ganges, Brahmaputra and Meghna. These spread their floods across one-third of the countryside each summer.

2 The great rivers carry soil sediment from the Himalayas which they deposit in a huge, constantly changing delta at the head of the Bay of Bengal. They bring the fertility which supports 110 million of the poorest people on earth and they can also bring disaster to this low-lying land. The raw power of these unstable rivers is difficult to comprehend. Just one breach of the right bank of the Brahmaputra in the 1988 floods inundated 1000 square kilometres of farmland.

3 For much of the year there is too little water. When the monsoon breaks, the flat landscape changes completely. Boats replace bicycles as the means of local transport and deepwater rice flourishes with the rising floodwaters. All of this is essential for the farming season. But when rainfall is exceptional and floodwaters rise higher than normal, the effects can devastate.

4 The farmers of Bangladesh are adept at making the most of their tiny plots of land. But with 11.6 people per cultivable hectare they are already at the extreme. Increased food production in an already hungry land means investing in dry-season agriculture. And this means protection from the floods.

5 After the disastrous floods in 1988 the Bangladesh government sought to determine whether modern engineering techniques and computer-aided technology could solve the problem. Aid organisations of all shapes and sizes offered flood-control assistance. When the reports were presented to the Bangladesh government in 1989, the advice was somewhat conflicting.

6 The French proposal was for embankments up to seven metres high to be built along the length of all the major rivers. They estimated the cost at $10 000 million up front and $150 million for annual repair and maintenance. Such expenditure would plunge the country into massive debt and divert money from other programmes.

7 By no means all the potential investors thought this was the answer. In the end the World Bank was asked to formulate an action plan. They did so, unveiling it in London in December 1989, and the $150 million needed for pilot schemes immediately became oversubscribed. The plan envisages as a first step finding out what social and technical problems the embankments would cause.

8 Many informed observers are extremely sceptical about the scheme. Despite assurances from the World Bank's Vice-President for Asia, Atilla Karaosmanoglu, that 'the people of Bangladesh will be consulted at every stage', the British aid agencies involved in disaster relief after the 1988 floods do not believe that people at the grass roots will be adequately involved. By what line of communication can the planners conceivably consult the poor?

9 Steve Jones, the European Community's advisor on the action-plan team says that the embankments are bound to have a huge social impact. Under the French proposal, around 20 000 hectares of land would be requisitioned and 180 000 people affected. Some households would lose everything, adding their numbers to Bangladesh's already burgeoning landless population.

10 Jones also points out that the embankments will take decades to complete and other flood-protection measures – improved flood warning, better disaster management – will be needed.

11 No-one knows more about managing the flood waters than the Bangladeshi people who live perched above them and whose welfare depends upon them. And it is essential that 'experts' brought in to help should be ready to learn from the existing 'experts'. Their ingenuity includes floating hen coops and mesh fences to stop fish escaping from flooded fish ponds. Ideas like these could be more widely promoted.

12 Meanwhile there will be profound environmental effects from canalizing such vast bodies of water. Every step forward on the grand embankment plan will have to be watched with care.

Annette Bingham is a specialist in water issues and Asian affairs.

Questions 8-18

The reading passage, **The grand embankment**, has 12 paragraphs. For each paragraph find a matching summary from the box below. Write only ONE letter in each space. Note that there are more summaries than paragraphs.

The first one has been done as an example.

		Paragraph	Your answers
A	An expensive proposal	1	Example: C
B	Doubts about Bangladeshi involvement		
C	The strong influence of water in Bangladesh	8 2	_____
		9 3	_____
D	Disastrous floods	10 4	_____
E	The plan's effect on people	11 5	_____
F	Time and other problems	12 6	_____
G	Advice from many groups on flood control	13 7	_____
		14 8	_____
H	Environmental effects of the plan	15 9	_____
I	The good and bad effects of rivers on Bangladesh	16 10	_____
J	Over-population problems	17 11	_____
K	Poor farming techniques	18 12	_____
L	The effect of water changes with the seasons		
M	Local expertise		
N	Putting the proposal into effect		

Writing

You should spend no more than 15 minutes on this task.

The United Nations International Drinking Water Supply and Sanitation Decade was launched in 1980 to provide 'water and sanitation for all by 1990'. The tables below show changes in water supply and sanitation levels during that decade.

TASK **Write a short report describing the changes in water supply and sanitation between 1980 and 1990. To what extent did the U.N. achieve its aims?**

Make sure the report is:

1 relevant to the question and
2 well organised.

You should write at least 100 words.

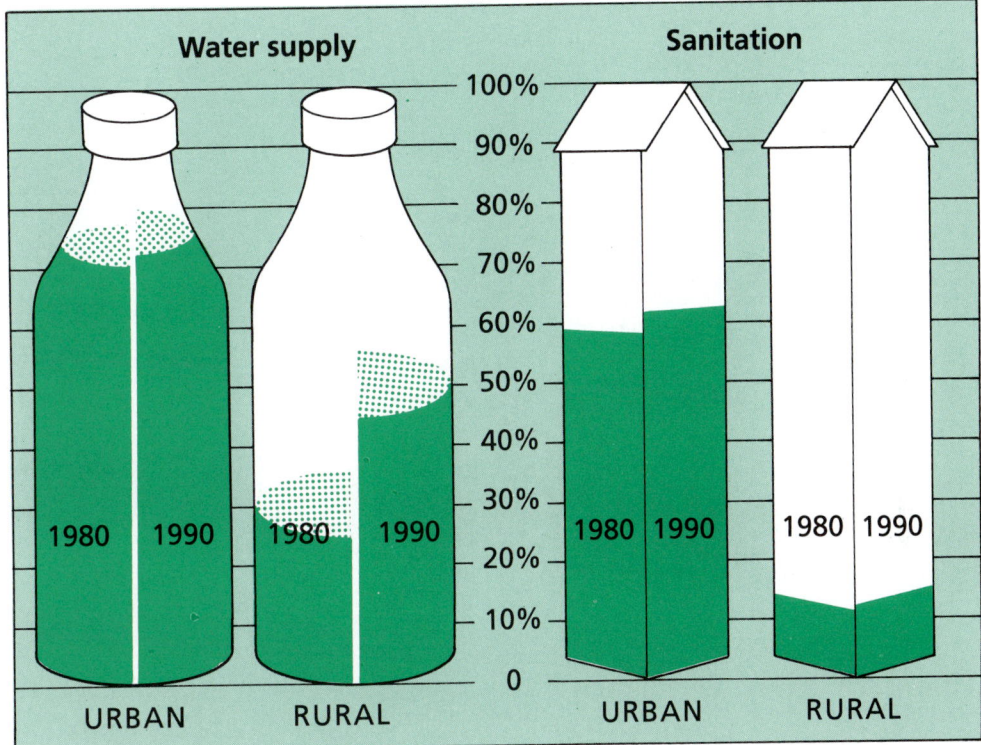

▶ L i s t e n i n g

Listen to this job interview, and fill the gaps numbered **1-10**.

WILLIAMS ENGINEERING Applicant details

Surname		Robinson
First name(s)	1	
Address	2	
		Prestwich
		Manchester
Telephone	3	
Date of birth	4	
Marital status	5	
Qualifications:		
'A' Levels	6	
Degree subject	7	
Special subject		Water Management
Institution		Sheffield University
Work experience:		
Post		Irrigation project engineer
Employer	8	
Length of service	9	
Post	10	
Employer		Latimer Engineering
Length of service		1988 to present

Speaking

Now 'interview' your partner, and fill in the necessary information about him or her on the applicant details form below.

Applicant details

Surname _____

First name(s) _____

Address _____

_____

_____

Telephone _____

Date of birth _____

Marital status _____

Qualifications:

Secondary _____

_____

_____

Degree subject _____

Special subject _____

Institution _____

Work experience:

Post _____

Employer _____

Length of service _____

Post _____

Employer _____

Length of service _____

▶ K e y   a n d   f e e d b a c k

Reading

The grand embankment

1   110 million

2   The French

3   A (World Bank) Action Plan

How did you answer these three questions? Did you:
- read every word of the text until you found answers
- or look quickly up, down and over the whole text?

See SKILLS FOCUS in this unit - *Scan Reading* on page 27.

In question 5, high cost is the **disadvantage;** the criticisms come *after* implementation of the proposal. So the order of the **question** can help you!

4   E

5   G

6   A

7   F

8   I

9   L

10   J

11   G

12   A

13   N

14   B

15   E

16   F

17   M

18   H

How did you answer questions 8-18? Did you read all the summaries first, or read the particular paragraph first and then look through the summaries?

Here's a method which works well:

> Look quickly through the list of summaries.
>
> ⬇
>
> Read a paragraph of the text.
>
> ⬇
>
> Find its matching summary from the box.
>
> ⬇
>
> Write the letter in the space.

If you choose a summary and then look for its matching paragraph, you'll have to read the whole text again and again. When you find a paragraph difficult to match with a summary, leave it, and go back to it at the end. Still can't answer it? *Write one of the remaining choices.* A final point: two summaries are not used – although the passage mentions farming, it says nothing about poor farming; *adept* in paragraph 4 means *skilled.*

> **General:** How did you handle *timing?* Did you have enough time? If not, what can you do next time to organise yourself better?

Writing

How did you plan your answer? Did you underline the key words in the question? Notice that the task asked you to do TWO things, 1) to describe changes, and 2) to assess the UN's achievement. Both should have been in your answer. Did you leave a couple of minutes for checking?

Here are three possible ways of organising an answer to this question.

1

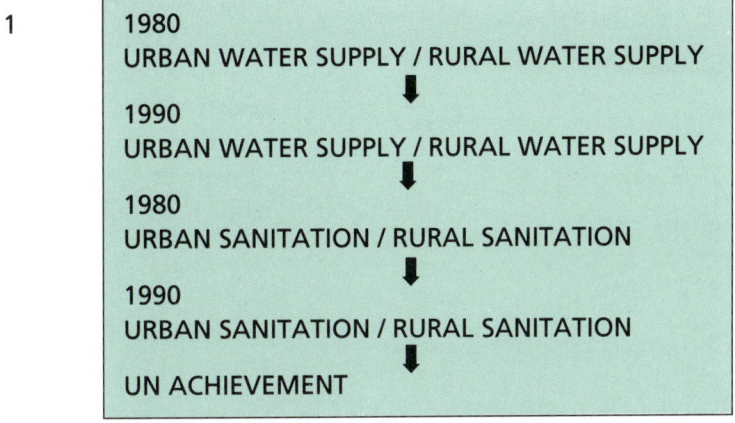

2

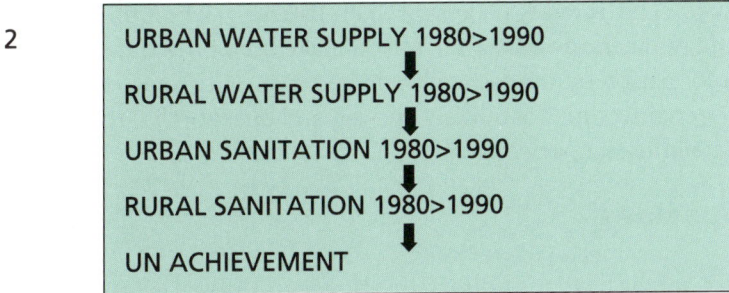

3

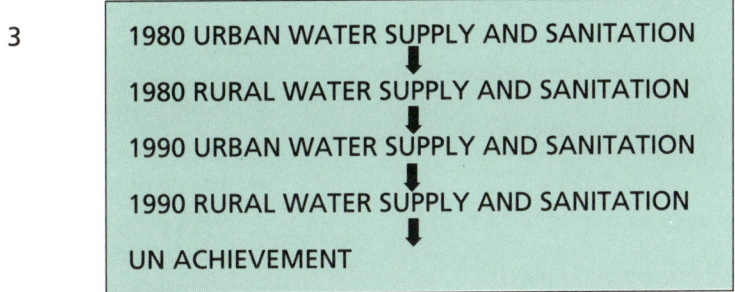

Which of the three do you like most? Which least? Why?

Organisation 2 answers the question the most precisely by presenting *changes* throughout.

Organisation 1 compares urban and rural rather than changes, while Organisation 3 fails to present changes until about half-way through the answer!

See SKILLS FOCUS in this unit - *Writing: Describing and Analysing Tables and Charts*, on page 29.

Listening

1	Steven	'Stephen' is *not* acceptable.
2	12 Dynevor Gardens	
3	483 250	
4	12 July 1961	You could write the date in a different order or style.
5	single	We never write 'not married' on a written form.
6	geography, maths, physics	All three (in any order) for 1 mark.
7	engineering	'Engineer' is *not* acceptable – this is a job title, not a subject.
8	the Chinese Government	
9	2 years	
10	(project) research assistant	

If you had difficulties, think about why. Were you trying to understand every word? This is rarely necessary when listening; when filling in a form, key words and numbers are enough. Did you make use of the time before listening? Information on the form allowed you to predict some of the answers, e.g. question 7 – engineering was a likely answer, and question 5 – there are only limited possibilities, married or single.

Speaking

You might have used direct questions like these in your interview:

What's your first name/surname?

Where do you live/What's your address?

What's your telephone number?

When were you born?

Are you married?

What qualifications have you got?

What do you do? (=What's your job?)

What work experience have you got?

How long have you worked for......?

There are other ways of asking questions.

Listen to the interview on tape again, and look at the TAPESCRIPT on p.138. Underline the interviewer's questions. Notice:
- his use of question tags; 'It's Mr Robinson, *isn't it*?'
  Use tag questions in your IELTS interview if you are *very* familiar with their form and usage: if not, avoid them, as it is very easy to make mistakes.
- his use of '*What about...?*'; it helps you to avoid using the same form of question again and again.
- that he asks *extra* questions not demanded by the task, about the wedding and the landlord, for example.

In the IELTS interview, extra, follow-up questions can help to demonstrate your communicative ability.

Skills Focus
Scan Reading

Sometimes when reading we know the kind of information we are looking for. For example, in question 1, page 18, you know you have to look for a number; in question **3,** you need to look for 'London' or '1989', and the answer will be close by. We don't need to *read* to find this information, rather, our eyes search across, up, down, and around the text. This skill is called 'scanning'. Think about how you look up a word in a dictionary. You *scan* the page to find the word you are looking for, you don't read the page. The most important thing about scanning is *speed*. We do it *quickly*.

Practice 1

Answer questions **1-4** as quickly as possible using the text below. Use your watch to time yourself. It should take you 1 minute.

1 How much of the human body is water?
2 How much water does the average person use for bathing?
3 How many people die per day from diseases related to dirty water?
4 How many litres of water does it take to make one pair of leather shoes?

The human body is about 65 per cent water. If you stopped drinking water (or drinks and food containing water) you would die within three or four days. But the water you drink must be clean.

Each day an average person uses the following amounts of water:

Toilet flushing	35 litres
Cooking and drinking	30 litres
Bathing	30 litres
Using a shower	12-20 litres

The average daily total per person is 140 litres. The average family uses 480 litres of water a day.

Water can carry diseases. According to a recent report published by the United Nations, every day throughout the world about 25 000 people die from diseases related to dirty water.

It takes 31 600 litres of water to make one car and 4124 litres to make one tonne of steel. It takes 53 litres of water to make one pair of leather shoes and 9 litres of water to make every comic that you read.

Practice 2

Before you answer the following questions, decide what kind of answer, or which words from the question, you are looking for. Then answer the questions. You have 2 minutes.

1 Give two examples of cities which have no sewerage.
2 Where is half of household income spent on water?
3 What must Lagos inhabitants do on 'sanitation day'?
4 Where do more than 60% of Third World people live?
5 In the 1970s, how many people had no proper means of waste disposal?

Meanwhile, people in the Third World can only envy the levels of health risk faced by those of us who can turn on a tap or flush a toilet. Most cities in Africa and many in Asia – Dakar, Kinshasa and Chittagong, for example, have no sewerage of any kind. Streams, gullies and ditches are where most human excrement and household waste end up.

People draw their drinking water from a standpipe which only operates for a few hours each day. Women still wash clothes and bathe their children in a muddy stream. In Nairobi, Jakarta, Bangkok and elsewhere, families are forced to purchase water from a vendor, paying ten times the rate charged to houses with mains connections (in Khartoum it is 18 times more expensive). In some parts of Sudan, half of household income is spent on water.

As city populations rapidly expand, water and sanitation services are put under pressures unimaginable to those who build them. But at least fear of epidemic – repeating the terrible ravages of cholera in nineteenth-century Europe – encourages action in city halls. Lagos, for example, used to be a watchword for urban filth. Now there is a monthly 'sanitation day' on which moving around the city is banned: everyone must pick up a shovel and clean their neighbourhood.

But until very recently, the sanitary environment inhabited by more than 60 per cent of Third World people – the countryside – was left to take care of itself. The woman carrying her container to the well, washing her laundry in the stream, leaving her toddlers to squat in the compound, had never seen a pipeline nor a drain; no faucet graced her village square, let alone her own backyard. At the end of the 1970s, 1.2 billion people in the Third World were without a safe supply of drinking water and 1.6 billion without any proper means of waste disposal.

Skills Focus
Writing Describing and Analysing Tables and Charts

In this unit, you used information from a table to talk about changes. When you write a report about *changes*, you need to write about the following:

1 The kind of change (increase or decrease)
2 The period of time involved
and *sometimes*
3 A comparison of different sets of information.

Look at the ways we can talk about these things:
1

30
20
10
  0 ↗
	↘ 30
	20
	10
	  0

to increase to go up to rise	to decrease to go down to decline
an increase a rise	a decrease a fall a reduction

We can give more information about the increase, decrease or change:

verb + dramatically verb + significantly	↗ ↘	dramatic + noun significant + noun
verb + a little verb + slightly	↗ ↘	small + noun slight + noun

2

Between	1980	and	1990 ...
In	1980 ...		
Since	1980 ...		

3

In 1980	30% of rural dwellers	compared with 50% in 1990.
	had drinking water	whereas in 1990 50% had it.

More	urban	dwellers have a water supply than	rural	dwellers.
Fewer	rural		urban	

Practice 1

Use language from the boxes to complete the paragraph about the pie chart below.

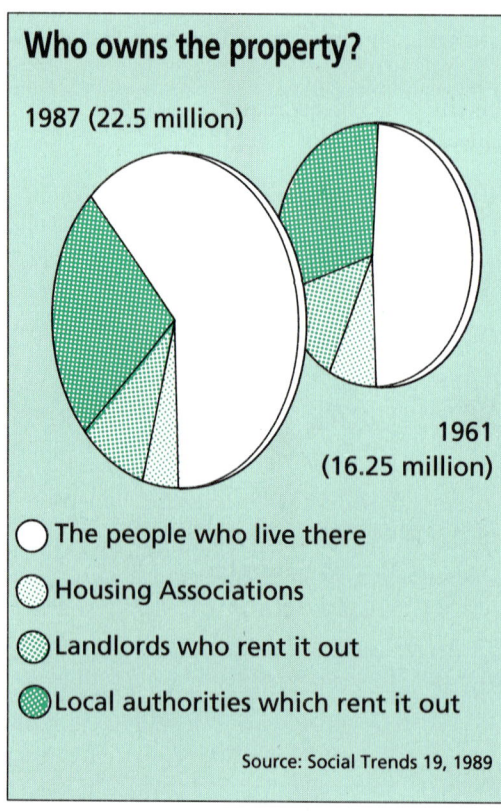

Who owns the property?

1987 (22.5 million)

1961
(16.25 million)

○ The people who live there

◐ Housing Associations

◑ Landlords who rent it out

● Local authorities which rent it out

Source: Social Trends 19, 1989

From the chart we can see that in _____ 16.25 million people owned property, _____ 22.5 million in 1987. This shows a _____ in the numbers of property owners. There has also been a _____ change in the number of people who live in their own homes. There seems to be no significant _____ in the number of houses rented out by local authorities. _____ people live in their own accommodation _____ in any other kind of accommodation.

Practice 2

Now write your own paragraph, using the pie chart below, to describe changes in shares of world manufacturing trade between 1973 and 1987.

(NIC = Newly Industrialising Country)

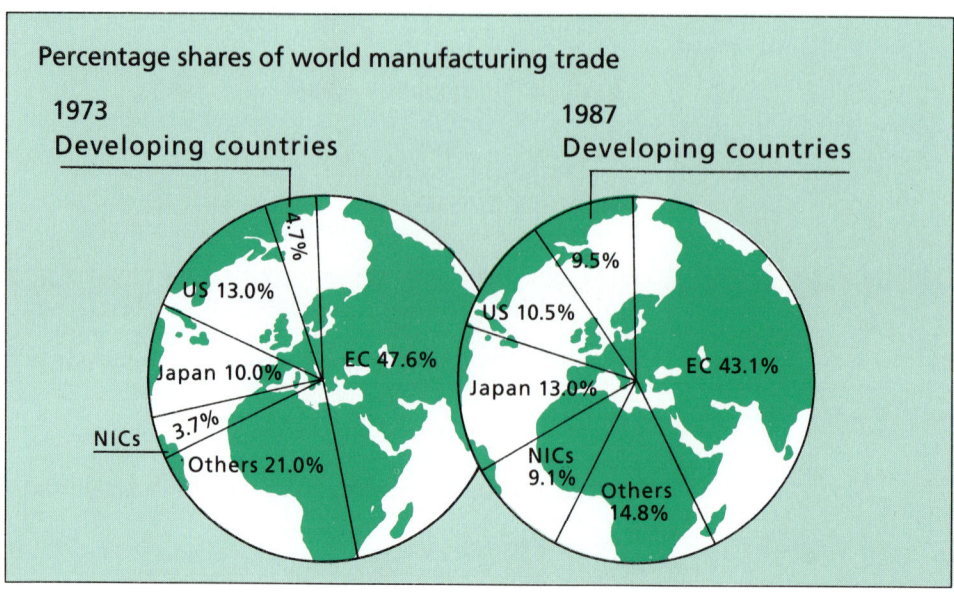

Percentage shares of world manufacturing trade

1973
Developing countries

1987
Developing countries

4.7%
US 13.0%
Japan 10.0%
NICs 3.7%
Others 21.0%
EC 47.6%

9.5%
US 10.5%
Japan 13.0%
NICs 9.1%
Others 14.8%
EC 43.1%

▶ **Reading** *You should spend 20 minutes on questions 1-15.*

Answer questions 1-15 using the reading passage.

Painful poultry

1 It's common practice in the poultry industry to amputate the beaks of chickens to prevent them pecking each other. Techniques of 'debeaking' vary, but in the UK it is performed on chicks when they are a few days old, and usually involves amputating one third of the upper part of the beak with a heated blade. The poultry industry has always assumed that chickens quickly recover, but evidence presented at the International Ornithological Congress in New Zealand suggests otherwise. Dr Michael Gentle, of the Institute of Animal Physiology and Genetics Research in Edinburgh, has shown that chickens can feel chronic pain weeks, and sometimes even months, after the operation.

2 Chickens have pain receptors in their beaks, and so slicing their beaks off with a hot knife must hurt them. What Dr Gentle has found is that the pain may be delayed, as is the case with human burn victims. 'The chickens are not in pain initially, but 24 hours later they show clear pain-related behaviour.' After the beak is amputated, the remaining stump may take two to four weeks to heal. But even then, pain may continue: the damaged nerves still grow, and may be 'abnormally and spontaneously active' (believed to be the cause of stump pain in human amputees). Even two months later, the stump is unusually sensitive to touch and temperature changes.

3 Many aspects of a chicken's behaviour also suggest that it experiences the long-term pain, and perhaps even the depression, typically felt by human amputees. In the first few weeks after debeaking, a chicken spends more time resting than usual. And even six weeks later, when the stump has healed over, a chicken avoids using its beak.

4 The habit of pecking each other doesn't necessarily start off as aggressive behaviour – it may simply be a substitute for pecking at litter – but it can quickly escalate once one bird is injured, and sometimes leads to the death of weaker birds.

5 Is debeaking really the solution, though? A very preliminary survey in Scotland, of two commercial laying breeds, found debeaking had no effect on the extent of feather and comb damage, or on body weights or the number of birds that died. A much more effective approach would be to remove the conditions – such as overcrowding and bright light, for example, that are known to contribute to feather-pecking and cannibalism. Where chickens really have to be kept in such conditions, a more sensible solution than debeaking, says Dr Gentle, would be to breed strains of chickens that don't peck each other.

Angela Turner

Questions 1-4

Complete the flowchart below with words from the reading passage.

	Your answer
Example:	
Chickens kept in poultry farms are often found .. (?)	*pecking each other*
⬇	
the practice of ..1..	_____
⬇	
carried out on young ..2..	_____
⬇	
a ..3.. is heated	_____
⬇	
..4.. of the beak is removed.	_____

Questions 5-9

The reading passage is divided into five paragraphs. From the list of headings (A-I) below, choose the most suitable heading for each paragraph, and write the letter in the space provided.

NB *There are more headings than paragraphs so you will not use all of them.*
You may use a heading more than once if you wish.

5 Paragraph 1 _____
6 Paragraph 2 _____
7 Paragraph 3 _____
8 Paragraph 4 _____
9 Paragraph 5 _____

A	Other effects of debeaking	F	The pecking habit
B	Chickens have feelings	G	Pain from amputation
C	Challenging an accepted practice	H	Improving the debeaking technique
D	Alternative solutions	I	Chickens are not aggressive
E	Methods of amputation		

Questions 10-15

10 What has been the poultry industry's assumption about the debeaking process, in relation to chicks?

_____

11 According to the reading passage, how long might chickens feel pain for after the operation?

_____

12 Dr Gentle twice compares the chickens with humans. Write the two categories of humans he compares them with.

1 _____   2 _____

13 What two pieces of evidence does Dr Gentle give to show that chickens suffer from long-term pain and even depression?

1 _____   2 _____

14 According to the passage one reason for the behaviour of pecking other chickens is ...
   A the need to peck at the ground in a natural habitat.
   B the need to assert dominance over weaker chickens.
   C the natural tendency for aggressive behaviour in chickens.
   D the frustration experienced by caged birds.

15 The author believes that ...
   A debeaking is necessary.
   B debeaking is sensible in certain conditions.
   C debeaking is not the right way to deal with the problem.
   D there is a link between debeaking and the number of chicken deaths.

W r i t i n g   *You should spend no more than 30 minutes on this task.*

Chickens are just one example of animals being kept in inadequate conditions for the benefit of human beings.

 **Write an essay for a university teacher on the following topic.**

Animals should not be used for the benefit of human beings, unless there is evidence that the animals do not suffer in any way.

You should write at least 150 words.

Where possible you should support your arguments with relevant ideas in the text, as well as using your own ideas, arguements and experience.

L i s t e n i n g

Listen to Clare and Jeremy talking about zoos, and decide if the following statements are TRUE, FALSE or if the required information is NOT MENTIONED. Write T, F, or NM in the space provided.

1 Clare thinks the presentation of the zoo is good. _____

2 According to Jeremy, many species survive in zoos which are now extinct in the wild. _____

3 The role of zoos is changing. _____

4 In Clare's opinion the idea of a zoo is old-fashioned. _____

5 Jeremy and Clare disagree about the importance of maintaining natural environments for animals. _____

6 Governments support zoos because they want to exploit natural environments. _____

7 Clare appreciates why people enjoy visiting zoos. _____

8 Jeremy argues that animals can benefit from being kept in newer types of zoo. _____

▶ Speaking

Spend a few minutes thinking about things that make your country's culture and customs special and different from other countries. Think about the following topics as well as other ideas you may have:

- Marriage: At what age?
  What kind of ceremony?
  What kind of preparations are necessary?

- Festivals: What are the major festivals each year?
  What do most people do at this time?
  Is there any special food?

- Transport: Is there a special kind of traditional transport?
  How do most people travel today?
  What about in the past?

- Folk tales
  and songs: Is there a group of stories or songs that all people know?
  How do you learn them?
  Do you know their origins?

Now pair up with a partner. If you are from two different countries, compare the customs and culture of both countries. If you are from the same country, discuss how you think your customs and culture are different from those of other countries.

Key and feedback

Reading

Painful poultry

1 debeaking
2 chicks/chickens
3 blade/knife
4 one third (of the upper part)

Notice that a 'flow chart' like this acts as a summary of the main points of a paragraph or passage.

5 C
6 G
7 A
8 F
9 D

10 It doesn't hurt /chickens quickly recover
11 months
12 1 burn victims   2 amputees
13 1 they spend more time resting
   2 they avoid using their beaks

You don't need to write whole sentences for this type of question, just key words.

14 A
15 C

Notice that question 15 asks about what the *author* believes.

Writing

This kind of question is asking for your opinion: do you agree with the statement, or not? However, a good answer will try to give arguments both *for* the statement and *against* it before stating a final opinion. The following essay does this, and we have given it two possible final opinions. Which is closest to *your* own opinion?

Animals are used by humans in many different ways: as food, for work, and often in research. This research often benefits humans, but may cause suffering for the animals. People say that animals can be used because humans have achieved dominance over them; moreover, if animals are not used for food, animal populations could grow out of control, which would cause many problems. Another point is that suffering inflicted on animals, especially during medical research, often prevents suffering to humans.

However, many people argue that it is wrong to cause suffering to animals for the benefit of humans. Meat is not a necessary part of our diet, and there are many healthy vegetarians around the world who prove this. Research carried out on animals is often not valid for human cases as an animal's physiology may be so different from that of a human. There are useful alternative forms of research available, including using cell cultures. Also, there is growing evidence about the pain suffered by animals, for example, the debeaked chicks in the reading passage.

Conclusion 1 In my opinion, it is necessary to use animals for the benefit of humans. Through their use, the quality of life for humans can be improved, and this is more important than the quality of life for animals.

Conclusion 2 I believe that animals should not be used for human gain. It is time to concentrate resources on developing alternative sources of food and methods of research, and allow animals a pain-free existence.

Listening

1 T
2 F
3 T
4 T
5 F
6 NM
7 F
8 T

If you don't hear an answer to a question, there's a good chance the answer is 'not mentioned'.

Speaking

What did you decide the main differences were between your culture and another culture? Did you use the present simple tense for talking about things that are always true? These topics are often very interesting for someone from a different culture – make sure you have plenty to say about them!

Skills Focus
Speaking about a topic in detail

In the speaking part of your test your interviewer may ask you to talk about something relevant to you.

We have started a list of general topics which could be discussed. Can you add a few more topics to the list?

Festivals and holidays	Economy and trade
Famous places	_____
Food	_____
Transport and communications	_____

Practice 1

If your interviewer asks you to tell him/her about one of these topics, he/she is expecting a *detailed* description. Look at the two dialogues below.

DIALOGUE 1

Interviewer: Can you tell me something about food in your country?
Candidate: Well, it's very famous.
Interviewer: Why is it famous exactly?
Candidate: Because it tastes very good.
Interviewer: Are there any special ingredients which make it taste good?
Candidate: Yes, of course.
Interviewer: Can you give me some examples?
Candidate: Well, we use spices a lot.

DIALOGUE 2

Interviewer: Can you tell me something about food in your country?
Candidate: Ah, yes. We're famous for our cooking. We have a lot of very spicy food which some foreigners find too hot, but the spices are essential for the flavours we like. We like meat a lot, but beans are also important in our dishes. Have you ever tried any of our food?

Dialogue 2 is the better one. Why?

Practice 2 'Just a Minute'

Work with a partner or group if possible. This is a game which can be quite fun in your own language as well as English. Ask your partner to choose *one* of the topics given in the list above. Your partner should time you; see if you can speak for one minute on this topic without stopping.

To make the game even harder your partner can stop you if you make any mistakes.

 ## Skills Focus
Listening for gist

When we listen, we do not need to understand every word to understand the main idea. When English is spoken the key words in a sentence are stressed, that is, strong, and the other words (usually grammar words) are weak, and therefore not easy to hear. The key words usually give us all the information we need.

Practice 1

Listen to the three short conversations and after each one write a telegram to a friend giving the main points. The first one is an example.

Example:

> **TELEGRAM**
>
> MUM/DAD, GETTING MARRIED! JULY?

1

> **TELEGRAM**
>
> MUM

2

> **TELEGRAM**
>
> MACPHERSON & CO

3

> **TELEGRAM**
>
> MUM/DAD

Practice 2

Now listen to three more extracts and decide who is speaking in each one. Choose from the list of options given in the box below.

tourist guide	policeman	teacher	doctor	friend	parent

▶ R e a d i n g *You are advised to spend about 20 minutes on questions 1-10.*

Questions 1-10

Answer these questions using the reading passage, **Road technology since the Romans**.

1 What were the *three* main factors the Romans took into account when building roads?

_____

_____

_____

2 Which diagram best illustrates Roman roads? Write **A,B,C,** or **D** in the space provided.

A  B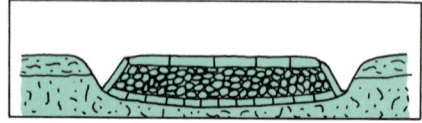

C 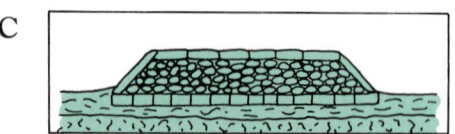 D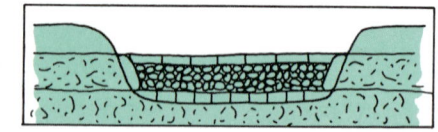

Your answer _____

The flowchart below represents the four stages in the 'next milestone in the history of roads' in paragraph 3. For each of the missing stages, match the new problem, action taken and result with the sentences in the box below. Write only *one* letter in each space.

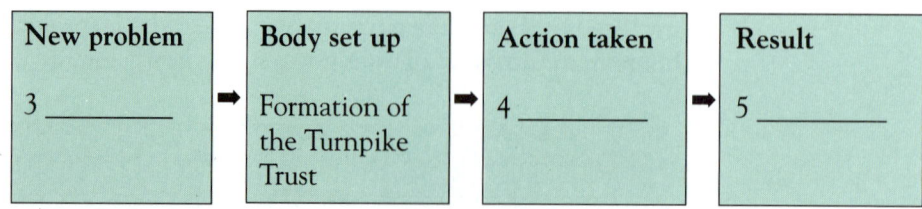

New problem	Body set up	Action taken	Result
3 _____	Formation of the Turnpike Trust	4 _____	5 _____

A	Roads became run down
B	Cash was raised
C	Lack of maintenance
D	Increasing numbers of wheeled vehicles wanting to go at higher speeds
E	Maintenance of roads in local areas

6 Which of the following best describes John McAdam's contribution to modern road technology? Write the letter in the space provided.

    A It is necessary to use a waterproof cover over the road.
    B It is necessary to prevent a road sinking.
    C It is necessary to keep the soil under the road dry.
    D It is necessary to limit the weight of traffic on a road.

Your answer _____

7 What is the advantage of a road surface made of tar and slag?

_____

8 In paragraph 6 what does 'a number of varieties' refer to?

_____

9 What are the four layers in the new 'upside down design'?

    i   _____
    ii   _____
    iii _____
    iv _____

10 What could prevent a clay sub-grade material clogging the sub-base?

_____

Road technology since the Romans

Important principles of road building were known to the Romans. How has technology developed since then?

1 Between 43 AD and 81 AD Roman Britain acquired a 6000 km network of technically advanced, hard wearing and straight highways linking towns of importance. Today Britain's motorway system is only half that length. The basic Roman philosophy of building a road to cope with different types and volumes of vehicles and using local materials where possible still applies today.

2 Roman roads were cambered with ditches on either side and built on embankments to give them a properly drained base. A surfacing layer of small stones was used over gravel or larger stones, although some Roman roads were covered with large paving flags, which is where the term 'pavement' originates.

3 Once the Romans left Britain, its roads fell into ruin through lack of maintenance. They became run down, dusty highways in the summer and quagmires in the winter. It seems that the next milestone in the history of roads was not until the 18th and 19th centuries, with the advent of the Turnpike Trust. This raised cash for necessary maintenance in local areas to cope with the increasing numbers of wheeled vehicles, coaches and carriages wishing to travel at faster speeds.

4 In 1816 John McAdam observed that it was the native soil that supported the weight of traffic which, when dry, would carry any weight without sinking. He advised that the native soil be made dry and a covering impenetrable to rain be placed over it. However, road maintenance was not given much priority due to the popularity of the railways, until the motor car superseded the horse and cart. Cars, however, accentuated the problem of dust, described by the medical journal *'The Lancet'* in 1907 as 'the greatest modern plague'.

5 Like so many other scientific advances, the solution came by accident. Tar mixed with stone had been used in footpaths in certain parts of Britain in 1832, and tarred gravel was applied to roads in Nottingham in 1869, but the biggest breakthrough came in 1901. A surveyor called E. Purnell Hooley was visiting Denby Iron Works near Derby when he noticed a dust-free length of road produced by a burst tar barrel. The resulting pool of tar had been covered with ironworks slag. Hooley experimented with blending hot slag and tar as a byproduct from the coal industry and in 1902 patented the process produced by a company known as Tar MacAdam Syndicate Ltd. The company's name was later changed to Tarmac.

6 Nowadays, blacktop materials are made up of bitumen from oil which is blended with rock, gravel or slag. A number of varieties have evolved for different uses in road construction, including hot-rolled asphalt for surfacing major roads, dense bitumen macadam for lower layers of a road and open-textured macadam. Modern surfaces are bituminous-bound, graded stone supplied as a premix. Binders themselves have undergone technical developments. They are customised, ranging from soft to very hard to suit the traffic flow.

7 To accommodate higher traffic levels, either the thickness of the road must be increased or the materials improved. Hence the introduction within the last 10 years of heavy duty madacam in the road base which is three times as stiff as the dense bitumen and aggregrate mix.

8 Alternatively, the structural design can be changed. For example, on an experimental reconstruction section of the M6 at Bescot, West Midlands, the heavy duty 'upside-down design' was introduced in the 1980s. Here, rolled asphalt overlays a thinner than normal road-base macadam, over a second rolled asphalt layer, all of which lie on a sub-base which is again thinner than normal. This structure is thought to perform well due to the lower rolled asphalt layer being more resistant to deformation and inhibiting cracking at the bottom of the road base.

9 Another innovative idea is the use of geotextiles. In research geotextiles are being placed between the sub-grade soil and a drainage layer beneath the sub-base. The sub-grade material is often clay and in the absence of the geotextile could, over time, clog the sub-base and reduce its efficienty as a drainage layer. But geotextiles can also have structural uses, and could provide improved resistance to cracking and rutting in roads.

Writing   *You should spend no more than 15 minutes on this task.*

Everybody uses taps every day. The diagram below shows how a tap works.

TASK

As a class assignment you have been asked to write a description of how a tap works.

Using the diagram below write a description of the tap and how it is used to allow water to flow.

Make sure your description is:

1   relevant to the question and
2   well organised.

You should write at least 100 words.

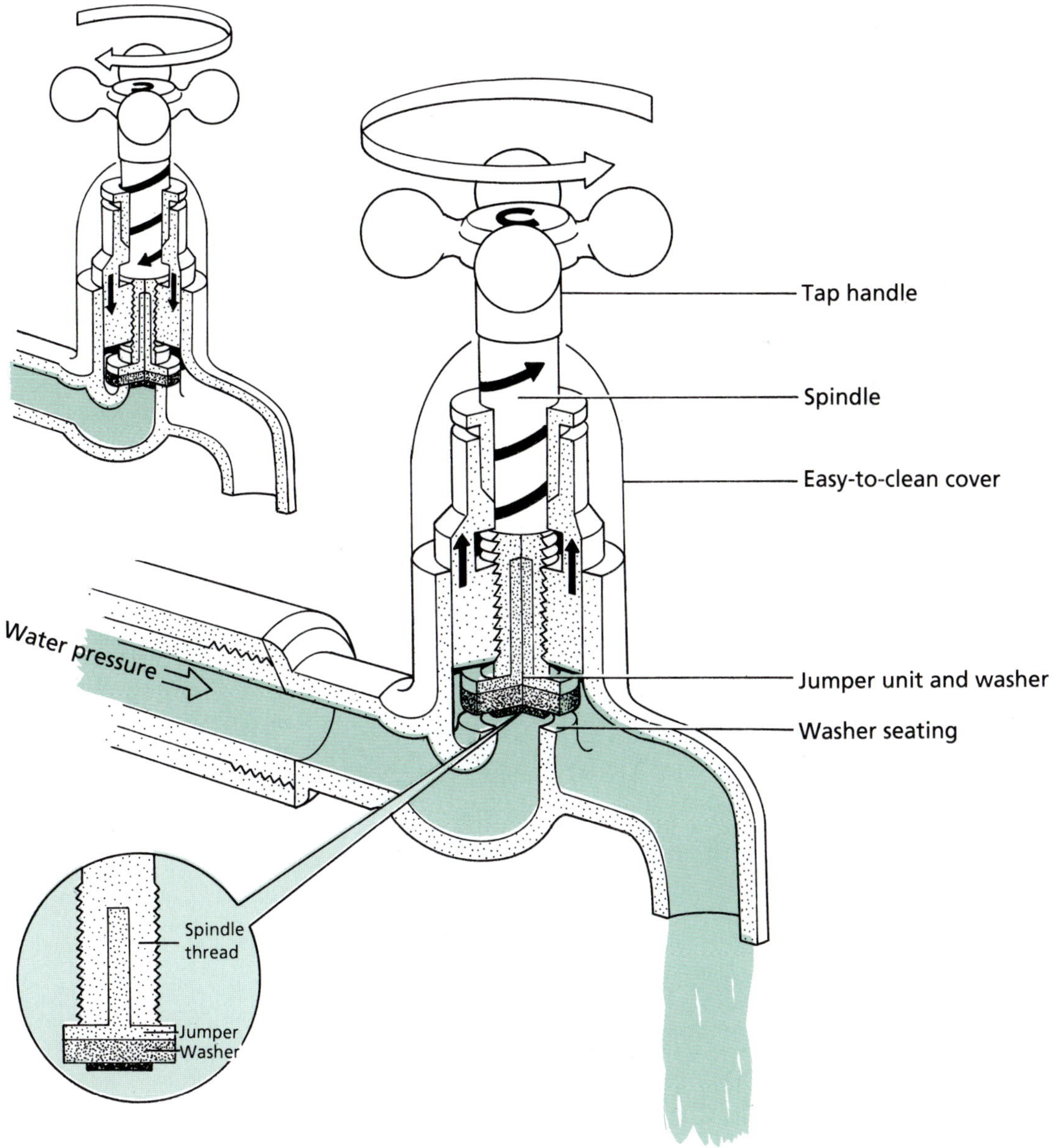

Tap handle

Spindle

Easy-to-clean cover

Water pressure →

Jumper unit and washer

Washer seating

Spindle thread

Jumper Washer

Listening

As you listen to the recording fill in the spaces numbered
1-10 to complete the notes below.

Frank is reading *New Scientist* magazine, which is a science magazine aimed at

1 _____ people rather than scientists. It has stories on

2 _____ issues as well as new breakthroughs in 3 _____.

One story in this week's magazine is about a new kind of telephone. You can

4 _____ the person as well as 5 _____ them. This new

videophone is different from the first ones because the image is in

6 _____ and moving. The new machine costs several thousands of pounds

compared to 7 _____ hundreds for the first, black and white, ones.

The clients the telephone company are expecting to buy the videophone, are

mostly businesses with 8 _____ contacts. Of course the contacts also have

to have a 9 _____, but if they have, a lot of travel can be avoided. The

telephone company might be wrong – people might 10 _____ meeting

face-to-face.

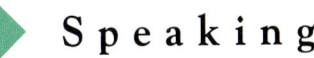

Speaking

On the tape you will hear two people explaining how to do something.

1 The first time you listen, decide what they are explaining.

2 Now listen again, and decide which of the two descriptions is clearer. Why is it clearer? Make some notes of the features which help you to understand it.

3 Look at the KEY AND FEEDBACK on page 46, and compare the notes there to your own.

4 Work with a partner or group. (If you are alone, record yourself to compare with the good description you have heard.)

Think of something to explain. Possible topics:

- How to play a sport / game

- Application procedures (job, college, club)

- How to use a piece of equipment

- How to borrow a book from a library

Without telling your partner(s) your topic, give an explanation of how to do / use it; they should decide what it is you are explaining, and if possible tell you how clear they thought your explanation was.

Key and feedback

Reading

Road technology since the Romans

in any order:
1 types of vehicle
  volume of vehicles
  using local materials

2 A   Paragraph 2: the key words were 'embankments' and 'ditches on either side'.

3 D   Notice how the information in the text is not
4 B   arranged in the order of events: you need to
5 E   read carefully and think logically about cause and effect e.g. the problem of increasing volume of traffic comes before the creation of the Turnpike Trust which was set up to solve the problem.

6 C   Did you choose A? The important discovery by
7 it is dust-free   McAdam was to keep the soil dry: of course
8 blacktop materials   you need a waterproof cover to do this but his
in any order: contribution was the discovery.
9 i   sub-base
  ii   rolled asphalt layer
  iii road-base macadam
  iv rolled asphalt layer
10 geotextiles

Writing

There were TWO parts to the task: (**1**) to *describe* the parts of a tap and (**2**) to say *how* it operates. Did you include both in your answer? Although you only have 15 minutes for this type of question, it is worth spending a minute or two studying the diagram given and making sure you understand it.

For more help with this kind of question see SKILLS FOCUS in this unit - *Writing: Describing how something works*, on page 49.

Listening

1 ordinary
2 current
3 research
4 see
5 hear
6 colour
7 several
8 overseas
9 videophone
10 prefer

In this kind of exercise it is important to use the time given to you before listening to try to predict the kinds of words missing. For example, question 4 has a grammatical clue: 'can', a modal verb, is always followed by verb 1: in question 6, your knowledge could help you to

Speaking

Extract 1 described a registration procedure for new students at a school.
Extract 2 described how to play a board game.

Extract 1 was difficult to follow because the speaker did not present the information in an organised way and had to keep going back to mention things that she missed. In contrast, **Extract 2** was easy to follow because:

- the speaker ordered information logically, starting with the object of the game.
- the speaker used the construction 'you' + verb 1, e.g. 'you move by ...', very commonly used to give instructions in English.
- short sentences help to keep the message clear.

Skills Focus
Skim reading

Look at these three headings:

A Britain's modern motorway system
B Roman principles relevant today
C 6000 km of Roman roads

As quickly as possible decide which of the headings best matches the paragraph, taken from this unit's reading passage, below.

```
Between 43 AD and 81 AD Roman Britain acquired a 6000 km network of technically advanced, hard
wearing and straight highways linking towns of importance. Today Britain's motorway system is only
half that length. The basic Roman philosophy of building a road to cope with different types and
volumes of vehicles and using local materials where possible still applies today.
```

The main idea of the paragraph is best expressed by heading **B**. Notice that **A** and **C** focus only on isolated details.

Getting the main idea of a text or paragraph quickly is called *skim reading*. There are different ways of skim reading:

  i If you're very short of time or reading, for example, a newspaper article, you might just read the heading and the first sentence of each paragraph. This is often enough to give you a fair idea of the content.

  ii For texts that you have to understand more fully, you might run your eyes along all the lines of the text, trying to pick out the key words and ignore unknown words and 'grammar' words (e.g. to, and, is, the) which do not contribute to the main idea.

Practice 1

Choose any English text. Give yourself 10 seconds to skim through one paragraph. At the end of 10 seconds, stop looking at the text and note down as many key words (not grammar words!) from the text as you can remember.

This is easy to practise alone; an alternative is to skim a text quickly and then try to summarise its general meaning.

Practice 2

Time yourself. Try to do the following task in under 8 minutes.
Refer back to the reading passage in this unit. Skim each paragraph and choose the most suitable heading from the box below.

A chance discovery	A road material for the future
Stronger materials for heavier traffic	Structural varieties
The first development after the Romans	Varieties of blacktop material
Roman road technology	Roman principles relevant today
A new observation	

▶ Skills Focus
Writing   Describing how something works

In this unit you used a diagram to write a description of how something worked.

When we describe how something works, the first thing we do is describe the **component parts** of the machine or object. *After* we have done this we choose a logical starting place and build up our description of how it works from there.

Look at the diagram below of a hand razor. What are the component parts?

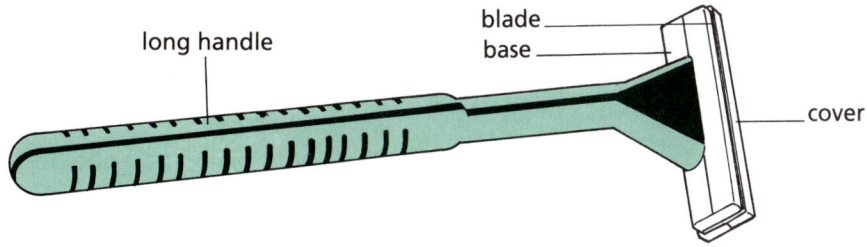

Here are some possible ways of describing the component parts.

A hand razor has four main parts:	a long handle, a base at the end of the
A hand razor is made up of	handle, a razor blade, and a cover to hold
A hand razor consists of	the blade in place.

Practice 1

Using this diagram which shows how a refrigerator works, fill in the gaps in the description given on the next page.

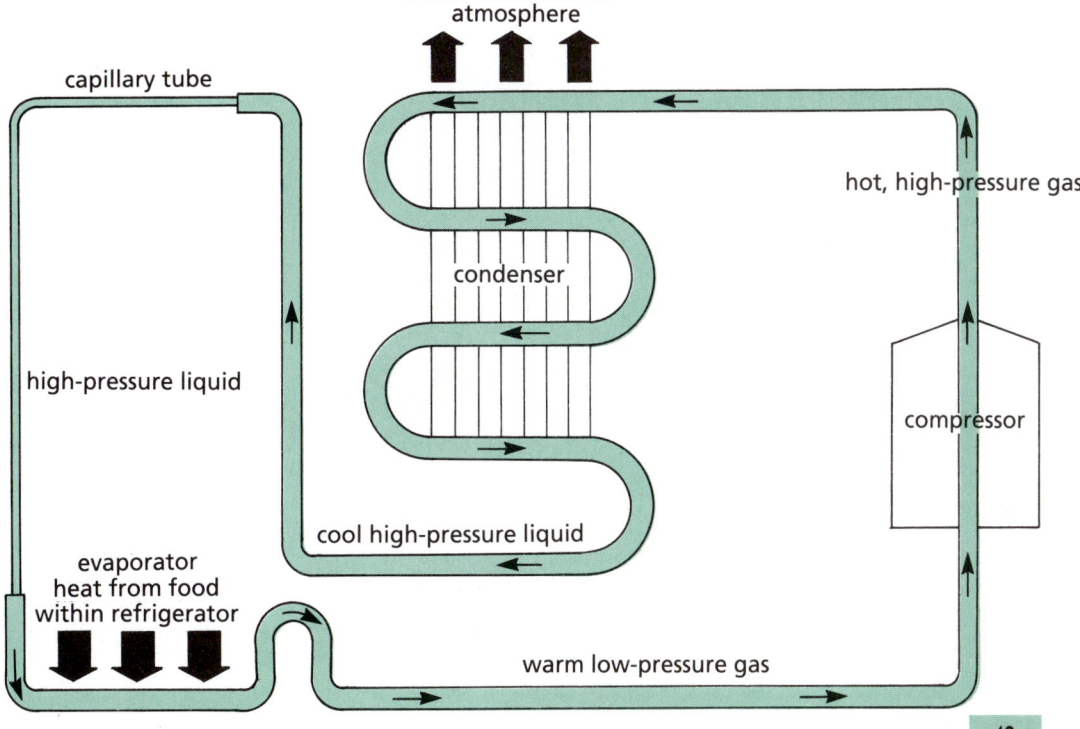

A description of how a refrigerator works.

A refrigerator is made up of a compressor, connected by a _____ to a

_____, which is connected by a _____ tube to an

_____.

The _____ compresses the _____ in the tube and this

resultant _____ enters the condenser.

Here, heat _____ to the atmosphere by radiation and the gas

_____ to become a cool high-pressure liquid which _____

through the capillary tube to the _____. _____ from food

within the refrigerator _____ by the liquid, so the temperature within

the refrigerator _____, and the liquid leaves the _____ as a

_____. This gas now _____ the

_____ and the process begins again.

Notice how the description follows a logical order, starting with the compressor
and moving round the component parts. Even when the object or machine does
not follow a cycle, you need to choose a starting point and follow from there. Also
notice that the passive voice is used when the main focus is on the object. For
example, in the above description, the sentence, *Heat from food within the
refrigerator is absorbed by the liquid ...* – here *heat* is the main focus, not *liquid*.

Practice 2

Now use the diagram of a camera below to write a description of its component
parts and how it works.

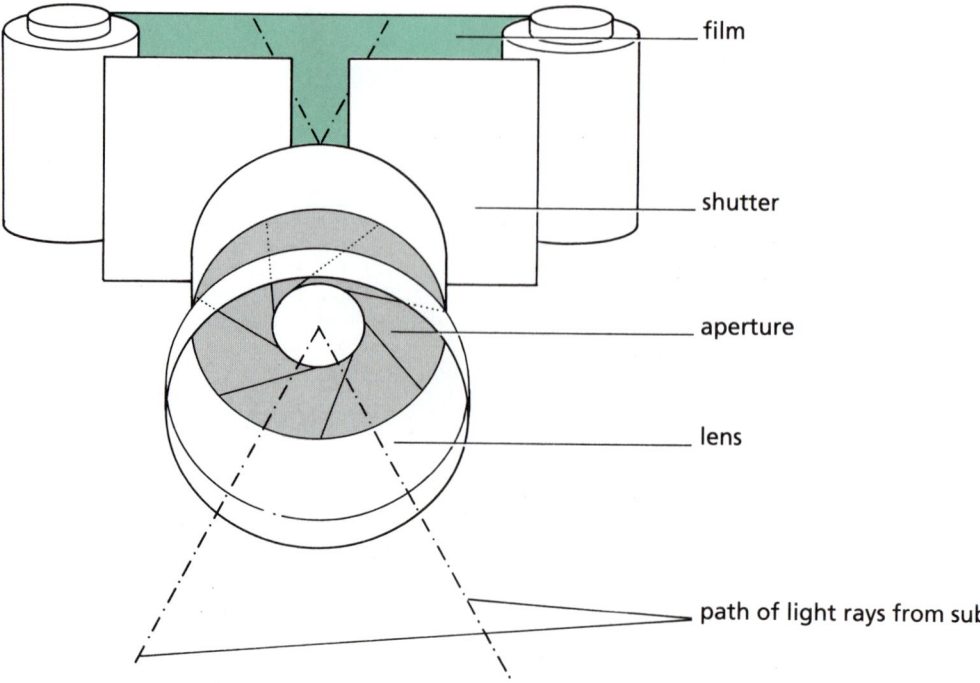

- film

- shutter

- aperture

- lens

- path of light rays from subject

▶ **R e a d i n g**   *You are advised to spend about 15 minutes on questions 1- 8.*

Part 1

Questions 1-5

Answer these questions using Reading Passage 1, **Recycling Britain**.

1 From paragraph 1, list the British target and the two things it will depend on.

Target _____   Depends on **1** _____

_____   **2** _____

2 What are the FOUR categories of British waste, according to the passage?

1 _____   3 _____

2 _____   4 _____

3 What part of British waste is best suited to recycling?   **Your answer**

_____

Questions **4** and **5** can be answered using statements from the box below. Decide which statement from the list **A-I** best answers each part of each question and write the letter in the space provided. There are more statements than you need.

4 What three projects could halve the amount of waste going to landfill sites?

1 _____   2 _____   3 _____

5 'This estimate makes two important assumptions.'
   (Paragraph 6). What are the two assumptions?

1 _____   2 _____

> **A** Government legislation
> **B** 'Bring' schemes
> **C** Creation of markets
> **D** Doorstep collections for newspapers
> **E** Plants for extracting metals
> **F** Improvement of products
> **G** 'Collect' schemes
> **H** Introduction of new technology by industry
> **I** Bottle banks

Reading Passage 1

Recycling Britain

1 By 2000, half the recoverable material in Britain's dustbins will be recycled – that, at least, was the target set last November by Chris Patten, Secretary of State for the Environment. But he gave no clues as to how we should go about achieving it. While recycling enthusiasts debate the relative merits of different collection systems, it will largely be new technology, and the opening up of new markets, that makes Patten's target attainable: a recycling scheme is successful only if manufacturers use the recovered materials in new products that people want to buy.

2 About half, by weight, of the contents of the typical British dustbin is made up of combustible materials. These materials comprise 33 per cent paper, 7 per cent plastics (a growing proportion), 4 per cent textiles and 8 per cent miscellaneous combustibles.

3 Of the rest, hard non-combustibles (metals and glass) each make up another 10 per cent, and 'putrescibles', such as potato peelings and cabbage stalks, account for 20 per cent, although this proportion is decreasing as people eat more pre-prepared foods. The final fraction is 'fines' – nameless dust. This mixture is useless to industry, and in Britain most of it is disposed of in landfill sites – suitable holes, such as worked-out quarries, in which the waste is buried under layers of soil and clay. That still leaves about 40 per cent of the mixture – glass containers, plastics, and some paper and metal containers – as relatively clean when discarded. This clean element is the main target for Britain's recyclers.

4 The first question, then, is how best to separate the clean element from the rest. The method of collection is important because manufacturers will not reuse collected material unless it is clean and available in sufficient quantities. A bewildering assortment of different collection schemes operates in the rest of Europe, and pilot schemes are now under way in many British cities including Leeds, Milton Keynes, Sheffield and Cardiff. Sheffield, Cardiff and Dundee are testing out alternatives as part of a government-monitored recycling project initiated last year by Friends of the Earth.

5 A realistic target for recycling mixed refuse is somewhere between 15 and 25 per cent by weight, according to researchers at the Department of Trade and Industry's Warren Spring Laboratory. This proportion would include metals and perhaps some glass. Statistics compiled by researchers at the University of East Anglia show that we could almost halve the total weight of domestic waste going to landfill by a combination of 'collect' schemes (such as doorstep collections for newspapers), 'bring' schemes (such as bottle banks) and plants for extracting metals.

6 This estimate makes two important assumptions. One is that the government will bring in legislation to encourage the creation of markets for products made from recycled materials, especially glass, paper and plastics. The other is that industry will continue to introduce new technology that will improve both the products and the techniques used to separate recoverable materials from mixed refuse.

Questions 6-8

Answer these questions using Reading Passage 1, **Recycling Britain**, above.

Choose which of the alternatives is the correct answer and put the appropriate letter in the space provided.

Your answers

6 In paragraph 1, the writer suggests that the Secretary of State for the Environment has:

   A   created an impossible target.
   B   provided a target without a method.
   C   given clear details of how to achieve a target.
   D   given manufacturers a target to aim for.   _____

7 'This mixture is useless to industry' (paragraph 3).
  This statement is:

   A   true for Britain but not for other countries.
   B   a matter of disagreement.
   C   the opinion of the author.
   D   an established fact.   _____

8 According to the text, recycling is only possible when:

    A there is enough clean material.
    B there is a small amount of clean material.
    C it is monitored by the government.
    D different collection schemes operate.

Part 2

You are advised to spend about 15 minutes on questions 9-15.

Questions 9-15

Look at Reading Passage 2, **Recycling Plastics**, on the next page. You will see that eight phrases have been left out. Decide which phrase from the list **A-L** below should go in each gap and write the letter in the space provided. Note that there are more phrases than gaps. The first one has been done for you as an example.

Your answers

A is characteristic of a different plastic.	
B developed their own compatibilisers.	**Example:** _____D_____
C which has never been achieved despite substantial government investment in research.	9 _____
D often used in wrappers and containers.	10 _____
E they could be used in high-grade, high-cost applications such as car bumpers.	11 _____
	12 _____
F it does not have sufficient rigidity.	13 _____
G for example, car bumpers made from one material instead of up to seven.	14 _____
H always been sceptical about recycling plastics.	15 _____
I as manufacturers do not want to be seen to be using recycled plastics in their quality products.	
J for example, steel suspension systems and car bodies.	
K such as polythene that are not chemically cross-linked.	
L the different plastics in the mixture are not bonded at a molecular level.	

Reading Passage 2

Recycling Plastics

One of the most difficult wastes to recycle is mixed plastic, _____ (Example) Plastics manufacturers turn their own offcuts into granules that are melted down for reuse. They can also reuse any single, pure thermoplastic materials _____ 9 . The British firm Meyer-Newman of Gwent recycles complete telephones into new ones. But mixed plastics have unpredictable properties and low structural strengths because _____ 10 . So, it is difficult to make a material with good and predictable properties from mixed plastics waste.

In the grip of the octopus

One answer is the compatabiliser. This is an octopus-like molecule in which each 'arm' represents a section of a different polymer, that in turn _____ 11 . Stirred into a mixture of molten plastics, each arm of the octopus grabs and reacts chemically with a molecule of one polymer in the mixture. The result is an alloy rather than a mixture. It is strong because of intra-molecular bonding and has highly predictable properties, so it is

potentially reusable.

During the past two or three years many plastics manufacturers have _____ _____ 12 . But perhaps the most advanced, 'Bennet', was produced independently two years ago, after 15 years of research, by the Dutch engineer Ben Van der Groep. His invention is already being used widely, largely in secret _____ _____ 13 .

Bennet is made up of short sections of several polymers representing the arms of the octopus, each able to link the molecules of a different polymer in the mixture. The reliable strength of the plastic 'alloys' made with Bennet suggests that _____ 14 .

The vehicles recycling industry is keen to recycle more plastics. Despite the environmental benefits, they fear that the steady increase in the use of unreclaimable plastics will soon make it uneconomic to recover vehicles for the metals they contain. Some car manufacturers, such as BMW and Mercedes, are now designing products and requesting components that are easier to recycle; _____ 15 .

Writing   *You should spend no more than 15 minutes on this task.*

Plastic litter is unsightly and appears never to rot away. Now chemists have produced a plastic that is made from sugar by bacteria, and, when discarded can be digested by other bacteria in the soil to form carbon dioxide.

TASK **As a class assignment you have been asked to write a description of how this plastic is produced and then broken down.**

Using the information in the diagram, write a description of the cycle.

You may use your own knowledge and experience in addition to the diagram.

Make sure your description is:

1 relevant to the question and
2 well organised.

You should write at least 100 words.

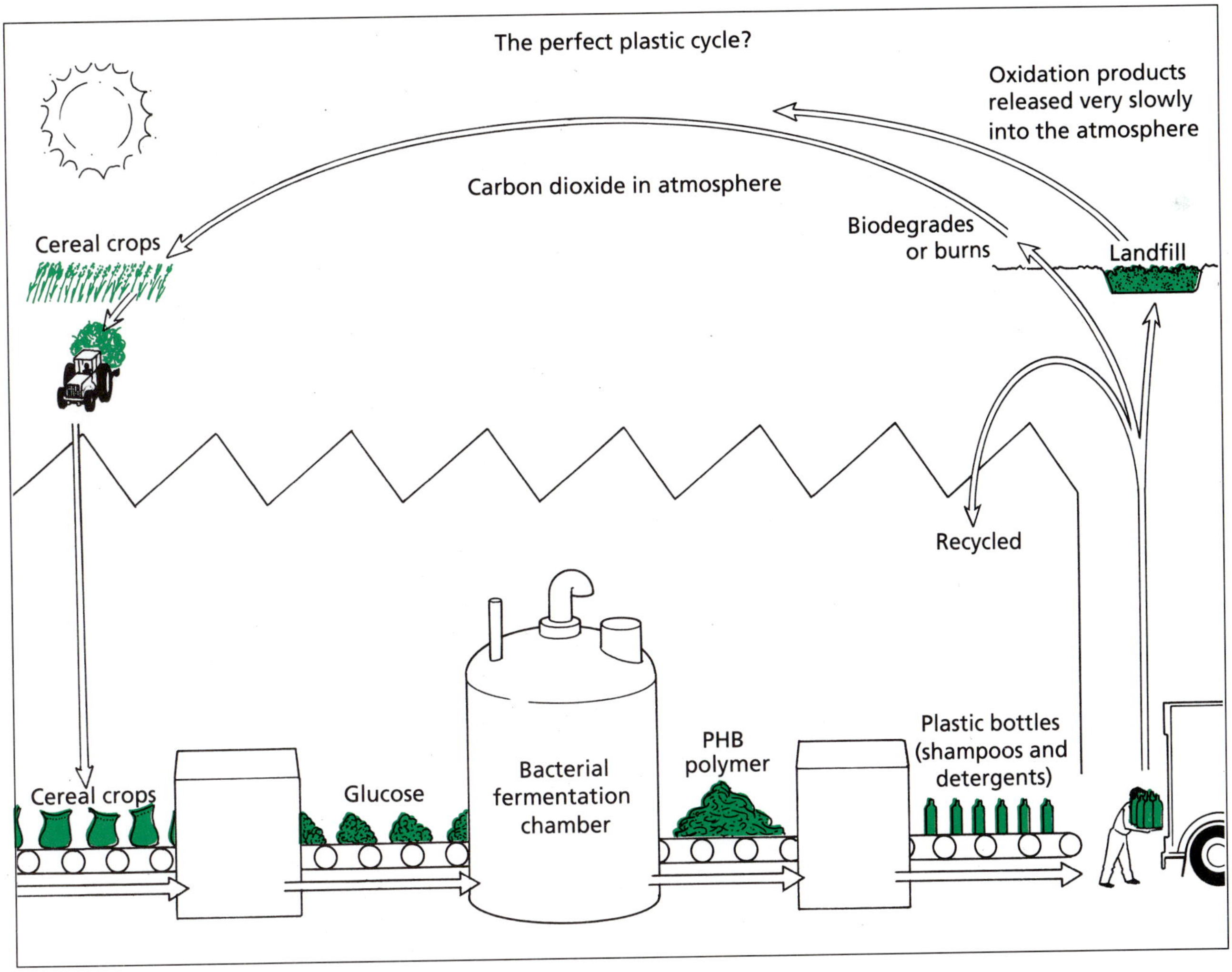

The perfect plastic cycle?

Oxidation products released very slowly into the atmosphere

Carbon dioxide in atmosphere

Cereal crops

Biodegrades or burns

Landfill

Recycled

Cereal crops

Glucose

Bacterial fermentation chamber

PHB polymer

Plastic bottles (shampoos and detergents)

Listening

Simon, Daniel and Gill are discussing plastic recycling. As you listen, answer questions **1-9** with a word or short phrase.

Example: Where are the students? _____ At university _____

1   How long does the first speaker think plastic sits before degrading?

    _____

2   How long does the second speaker think it takes?

    _____

3   What does Daniel say we are throwing away every time we throw away a bottle?

    _____

4   Where does Simon say people are most likely to put something they want to throw away?

    _____

5   Why does Gill think plastic bottles and containers are suitable for recycling?

    _____

6   What, according to Daniel, is the 'old idea' of recycling?

    _____

7   Why does Simon have to leave?

    _____

8   Where do Simon and Daniel agree to meet later?

    _____

9   Why won't Gill be able to come?

    _____

Speaking

Work with a partner. One of you look at **Role Card A**, and the other at
Role Card B.

Role Card A

Your partner is a member of Globewatch, an environmental pressure group.
You think you would like to join, but want more information. Ask your
partner questions to find out as much as you can.

Some things to find out about:
        number of members
        membership cost
        joining procedure
        frequency of meetings
        location of meetings
        activities of group

Role Card B

You are a local member of Globewatch, an environmental pressure group. A
friend of yours would like to join. Answer his or her questions about the
organisation using the information below.

Membership:	£37 per annum
	£51 per annum for a couple
	£20 per annum for students
Joining:	application form from office – then send cheque
Meetings:	once a month at local members' houses
Number of members:	most local groups 150 – nationally 3000
Activities:	collection and recycling schemes; petitioning MPs; awareness-raising; fund-raising

Key and feedback

Reading

1 Recycling Britain

1   *Target* by 2000 half recoverable
     material recycled
     Depends on   1 new technology
                    2 new markets
     in any order:
2   1   combustible materials
     2   non-combustibles
     3   putrescibles
     4   fines
3   the clean element
in any order:
4   1 G 2 B 3 E
5   1 A 2 H
6   B
7   D
8   A

Notice the % figures referred
only to combustible waste, not
all British waste: you needed to
read beyond the second
paragraph.

This paragraph is a factual
description about British waste.

2 Recycling Plastics

9   K
10   L
11   A
12   B
13   I
14   E
15   G

Remember to use your
knowledge of grammar in this
type of question to make sure
the phrase you choose 'fits' the
space.

Did you choose J? Remember
the passage is about recycling
plastic not metal.

Writing

Look at this possible answer to the task.

> Cereal crops are transported from farms to a factory, where glucose is extracted. Then the glucose passes into a chamber where it is fermented by bacteria to produce a plastic substance called PHB polymer. This is used to manufacture plastic bottles, for example, for shampoos or detergents. After use, some of these bottles are recycled, some are placed in landfill sites, and some are disposed of randomly. The non-recycled bottles biodegrade and carbon dioxide is released very slowly into the atmosphere, and this is used by plants such as cereal crops to grow. These cereal crops are harvested and the cycle begins again.

Some points to notice:

The **passive** to describe a cycle or process: crops *are transported...*
                                                          glucose *is extracted...*

Sequencing words such as *then* or *after*.

Words **referring** back to something already mentioned:
                ...to a factory, *where*...
                ...PHB polymer. *This* is used to...

General to specific. The first time glucose is mentioned it is simply *glucose*, the second time we know which glucose is being mentioned so it becomes *the glucose*.

Listening

1 centuries
2 a couple of years (or two years)
3 the world's resources / oil
4 the dustbin
5 easily collectable (and reusable)
6 using again for the same purpose
7 he has a lecture
8 (the new bar in) George Street
9 She's playing squash.

Speaking

Notice that the words given on Role Card A are not necessarily the words you will use in your questions. For example, you would not say, *What's the frequency of meetings?* Here are some suitable questions:

                Could you tell me how much membership costs?
                How do I join?
                How often are the meetings?
                Where do they take place?
                And what sort of activities do they do?
                How many members are there?

Now see the SKILLS FOCUS in this unit - *Asking questions*, on page 60.

Skills Focus
Asking questions

You may have to *ask* your examiner questions in your speaking test as well as *answer* him / her. There are several different types of question in English. Look at the list of questions below and divide them into two groups.

1 *Do you live in Malaysia?*
2 *Could you tell me where the station is?*
3 *Where is the doctor's?*
4 *How much does membership cost?*
5 *Would you mind telling me where you live?*
6 *Can I ask you what your name is?*
7 *What's the time?*
8 *Can you tell me who the manager is?*
9 *Who did you see yesterday?*

Group A _____   Group B _____

Which group contains *direct* questions? Which *indirect*? We use indirect questions when *difficulty* is involved; we don't know the person we're talking to, or we need to be polite, or we're asking for something major.

Indirect questions use a phrase or expression followed by word order like a *statement*, NOT like a question:

Could/can you tell me
Would you mind telling me   what his name is?
Can I ask you
I wonder if you could tell me

(NOT what is his name?)

In most direct questions, an auxiliary verb comes before the subject; if there is no auxiliary verb we use **do/does/did**.

	AUX	SUBJ	VERB
Example: Where	do	you	live?
Why	has	he	left?

Look at the two dialogues below. Which do you prefer? Why?

A: Good morning. Would you mind telling me your name?

B: Robert Murray.

A: Thank you. And could you tell me when you were born?

B: 21 June 1958.

A: Right. Can I ask you what your address is?

A: Good morning. Would you mind telling me your name?

B: Robert Murray.

A: Thank you. When were you born?

B: 21 June 1958.

A: Right. And what's your address?

The second dialogue is better: initially an indirect question was used to establish politeness, then 'A' used a direct question. In fact, when we ask a series of questions we shorten questions more and more, for example:

What about your job?
And your work experience?

When a lot of questions are asked, using varied question types is more natural than repeating one type again and again.

Practice 1

Rewrite the following dialogue. There are both grammar mistakes and inappropriate question types.

Shop assistant:	*Good morning.*
Customer:	*Good morning. I wonder if can you help me? I'm looking for a pair of shoes.*
Shop assistant:	*Certainly. Can you tell me what style you would like?*
Customer:	*Yes, I want a flat pair that are comfortable for walking.*
Shop assistant:	*OK. Can you tell me what size you take?*
Customer:	*Six.*
Shop assistant:	*Right. Would you mind telling me what colour you prefer?*
Customer:	*Light brown, I think.*
Shop assistant:	*You like this pair?*

Practice 2

Write and practise a dialogue between a bank manager and a customer. The bank manager wants to find out the following things about the customer:

> full name
> address
> date of birth
> marital status
> job
> salary
> why the customer wants a loan

Remember to vary your question types!

Skills Focus
Listening for specific information

In Unit 3 SKILLS FOCUS - *Listening for gist*, page 39, you looked at how to listen for the main idea. Sometimes, however, we know what specific information we are listening for, for example, the exact score in a football match, or the time of a television programme. Often this specific information is a number, a time, a name or a place.

Consider the questions below taken from a listening test. Which questions require you to listen for the main idea (gist), and which require you to listen for a specific piece of information?

1 How many people were at the party?

2 Why didn't Sandra go to the party?

3 What time did the party start?

4 Why did most people feel that the party was a success?

5 Why didn't Peter agree?

Often specific information questions like numbers **1** and **3** above are easier to answer than gist questions because you can predict what kind of information you need to listen for. Here you know you need to listen for a number (in question **1**) and a time (in question **3**).

Practice

You are going to hear a short news broadcast. First look at the questions below and decide whether each answer will be a name, a place, a number or a time. Then listen and answer the questions.

Questions

1 What time was this news?

2 How many people are believed to have been killed in the gas explosion?

3 When were three aid workers killed?

4 Who won the cricket at Headingley?

5 Which river does the new bridge opened by Prince Andrew cross?

Remember to use the time *before* you listen in the IELTS test to predict what kind of information you need. See also the SKILLS FOCUS in the next unit - *Reading: Gap-filling tasks*, page 74.

▶ **R e a d i n g** *You are advised to spend 10 minutes on questions 1- 8.*

Part I

Questions 1-8

Below is a passage from a guide giving advice to foreign nationals living in Britain. Read the passage, then fill in each gap with ONE word from the box at the foot of the page. Write your answers in the spaces below the passage. The first one has been done as an example.

Losing your passport

If something has happened to your passport, ___**(Example)**___ your embassy at once and ask them to tell you all the documents that you will need to produce to be _____**1**_____ with a new one. This is most important because some embassies require extensive documentary proof of nationality, as well as proof of identity, such as driving licence, or credit cards. So take care that you are not wasting time and money when you can least _____**2**_____ either. If your passport has been lost or stolen, your embassy will want you to _____**3**_____ the incident to the police as soon as possible. When you do so, ask for the police reference number of your case as many of the embassies find this useful in following up your _____**4**_____ .

Similarly, take your passport number with you to the embassy, as this will accelerate your case. The size and number of the photographs that you will need will _____**5**_____ on your embassy, and some may even recommend a photographer. You should also confirm with embassy officials how much you will have to pay, and also in what _____**6**_____ it is to be paid.

Some of the embassies are prepared to issue on-the-spot emergency passports, requiring no more than your oath to claim your _____**7**_____ , but as a precaution you should investigate the requirements *before* you are actually _____**8**_____ to make an emergency request.

Your answers

Example:_____*inform*_____

1 _____

2 _____

3 _____

4 _____

5 _____

6 _____

7 _____

8 _____

afford	forced
answer	identity
applied	investigate
character	inform
claim	issued
considered	money
currency	report
depend	spend

Reading Part 2

No word for anxiety

You are advised to spend about 20 minutes on questions 9-24.

Questions 9-11

Answer these questions, using the reading passage, **No word for anxiety**. Write your answers beside the questions. The first one has been done as an example.

Example: Many Bangladeshis in Britain live in __Tower Hamlets__ .

9 In one word, 'duschinta' and 'udhbeg' roughly translate as

   _____ .

10 Learning to relax is normally compared with _____ .

11 Why do the writers think their rapport with the women happened so quickly?

   _____ .

Questions 12-15

Choose which of the alternatives is the correct answer and put the appropriate letter in the space provided.

Your answers

12 What is meant in paragraph 1 by 'colour blind'?

   A Not liking people from ethnic groups.
   B Giving specialised treatment to ethnic groups.
   C Unable to distinguish certain colours.
   D Not treating ethnic groups differently.   12 _____

13 The Bangladeshi women continued to visit their doctors because:

   A they were lonely and isolated.
   B the reasons for their problems were still there.
   C they were being prescribed drugs.
   D they were referred to mental health professionals.   13 _____

14 The standard approach to treating anxiety had to be changed because:

   A the cultural background of the women was very different from the standard one.
   B the Bangladeshis were exposed to racist harassment and language difficulties.
   C the Bangladeshi women asked them to change it.
   D the women could not relax.   14 _____

15 It is important to have bilingual ethnic staff because:

    A they can protect the people from racism.
    B people relate better to people of similar backgrounds.
    C of language problems.
    D they do not fall into the stereotype of assuming
       ethnic groups do not understand.

15 _____

No word for anxiety

Psychologists Aruna Mahtani and Afreeen Huq look back with mixed feelings on their special project for Bangladeshi women in Britain.

1 Our training as mental-health professionals is supposed to be 'colour blind'. That sounds fine but in practice it means that people from black and ethnic groups get a raw deal because their particular problems are seldom acknowledged. Even when they are provided for it usually amounts to their being dumped on the few professionals from black and ethnic groups.

2 So we decided to pilot a project involving Bangladeshi women from Tower Hamlets in the East End of London. The largest Bangladeshi community in Britain lives in Tower Hamlets – at least 40 000 people. Most migrated in the 1960s and 1970s. Adjustment was difficult and the transition from a rural to an inner-city setting was hardest for women. They found themselves confined indoors, isolated and without the networks of social support they were used to in Bangladesh.

3 Many of these women turned to their doctors with common symptoms of anxiety, such as palpitations, headaches, tearfulness, sleeping difficulties, chest pains, loss of appetite and lack of energy. They were usually prescribed tranquillizers or even placebos like ascorbic acid (Vitamin C). Since the underlying causes remained, the women visited their doctors with increasing frequency. And some were referred on to mental-health professionals like us.

4 We wanted to see how normal Western approaches to anxiety problems might work when applied across cultures. Our first step was to get an anxiety-management package translated. No easy task: there is no colloquial expression in Bangla for 'anxiety'. We used two approximations, dushchinta ('undue worries') and udhbeg (a word generally used only in its written form).

5 We knew we had to have a women-only group. A mixed one would have been unacceptable to both the women and their families. Bangladeshi women rarely go out alone. Their cultural background is that of a small rural community where women tend to go out with family members or neighbours. In Britain they are even less likely to go out due to fear of racist abuse and harassment, as well as language difficulties.

6 So many things in the standard approach had to be changed. We had to translate many of the usual examples – we would normally compare learning to relax with learning to drive, for instance, which would not have been culturally appropriate. At first we asked the women to rate, on a scale one to ten, the effect of relaxation on their level of anxiety. They found numbers an odd way of expressing how they were feeling. So we shifted our focus to words and talked of five stages from 'very good' to 'very bad'.

7 It was a pilot project, so there were shortcomings. We looked for too little back-up, naively taking on too much, like driving the women to and from the centre. We did not collect as much objective data as we might have done with a white group. We fell into the white stereotype of assuming that Bangladeshi women would find the use of various checklists and written records foreign. Perhaps racism has conditioned us to a greater extent than we expected.

8 But the rapport between us and the women in the group was instantaneous, probably because we share not just a language and culture but a common experience of racism. The importance of having bilingual and ethnic staff is clear.

9 We found that using a Western model across cultures has potential. But it needs political, financial and personal commitment. And the lack of response by the authorities in Tower Hamlets leads us to conclude that 'institutional' racism is very much alive and kicking.

Aruna Mahtani and Afreen Huq are clinical psychologists. Aruna Mahtani is co-author of *Transcultural Counselling in Action* (Sage).

Questions 16-24

The passage below is a summary of the reading passage, **No word for anxiety**. Decide which word should go in each gap and then write the letter in the space provided. Note that there are more words than gaps. Write only one letter in each space.

The first one has been done as an example.

A conditioned	**F** rapport	**K** records
B data	**G** transition	**L** rate
C allowance	**H** urban	**M** exposed
D acknowledged	**I** inform	**N** symptoms
E statistic	**J** translate	**O** rural

Summary of 'No word for anxiety'

People from black and ethnic groups frequently find that their problems are not __(Example)__. A project was piloted involving Bangladeshi women in inner-city London. Most came to the UK in the 60s and 70s from a ____16____ background. Particularly for women, this ____17____ has been very difficult to adjust to. Many of the women experienced common anxiety ____18____ and after visiting their doctors some were referred to clinical psychologists. First, the psychologists had to ____19____ an anxiety-management package. Then a women-only group was established. They asked the women to ____20____ in numbers the effect of relaxation on their anxiety level, but this was an odd concept for them so words were used instead. Being a pilot scheme, there were problems such as not having sufficient back-up and working too hard. They ended up with less ____21____ than with a white group. They made assumptions about Bangladeshi women's approach to keeping ____22____ and wondered if they were more ____23____ by racism than they expected. However, being of an ethnic group themselves led to a good ____24____ due to a shared language and exposure to racism.

Your answers

Example _____D_____

16 _____

17 _____

18 _____

19 _____

20 _____

21 _____

22 _____

23 _____

24 _____

W r i t i n g   *You should spend no more than 15 minutes on this task.*

Look again at the reading passage, **Losing your passport**. You are studying at a university in the north of England. Your passport has been stolen. Here is the form you filled in for the police:

Lost Passport Details   Police Reference Number: CX241

Passport number _A4847009X_

Date of issue _30/2/1987_   Date of expiry _29/2/1997_

Place lost _Leeds bus station_   Date and time lost _9/10/91 10.20_

TASK   **Write to your embassy in London, giving details of what happened and asking what you should do next.**

You should write at least 80 words. You do not need to write your address.

Begin:

Dear Sir/Madam,

Listening

Section 1 Questions 1-4

Decide which of the pictures best fits what you hear on the tape, and circle the letter beside that picture. We have done the first one for you.

Example: Where is the ticket office?

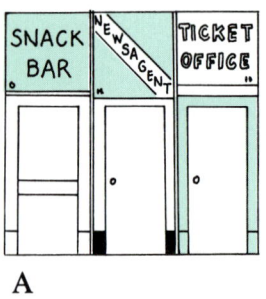
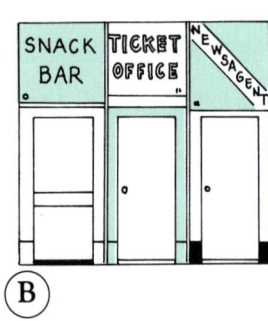

A   B   C   D

1 What is the situation when they arrive at the ticket office?

A   B   C   D

2 Which ticket do they buy?

A   B   C   D

3 What time is their train to Edinburgh?

A   B   C   D

4 Which sign do they follow?

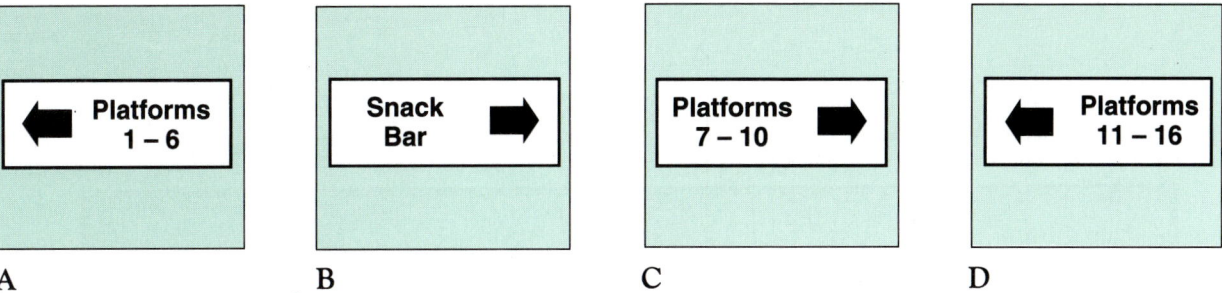

A   B   C   D

Section 2 Questions 5-10

Fill in the gaps numbered 5-10.

RAILWAY LOST PROPERTY FORM

Date __11th Aug.__

Surname	Adams
First name(s)	**5**
Address	21 Thames Drive
	6 ESSEX
Telephone	**7** 0702
Item lost	Camera
Description	**8** KA 10
(Include make and	
model if possible)	
Train	London/Edinburgh
Time of arrival	**9**
Customer notification	
(tick one) **10**	☐ by post ☐ by telephone
	☐ will call back to collect

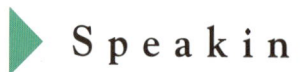 S p e a k i n g

Work with a partner. One of you look at **Role Card A,** and the other at **Role Card B.**

Role Card A

You are in Liverpool. You want to travel by train to Manchester to catch a plane. Student B has information about trains to Manchester.

Ask Student B questions to find out as many details as possible. It is now 11.00 am.

SOME THINGS TO FIND OUT:

- train times (departure and arrival)
- cost (single and return)
- reductions for students
- refreshment facilities
- platform number

Role Card B

You work in the information office at Liverpool train station. Use the information below to answer Student A's questions.

Liverpool to Manchester train timetable					Cost
		Platform			Standard single: £7.20
	10	11	10	10	Standard return: £12.80
Liverpool: deps	11.15	11.23 *	12.20	12.45	Student single: £5.60
Manchester: arr	12.00	11.55	12.50	13.30	Student return: £10.20

Bus connections to airport are hourly, on the hour.

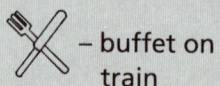 – buffet on train

★ – express train

Key and feedback

Reading

1   Losing your passport

1 issued
2 afford
3 report
4 claim
5 depend
6 currency
7 identity
8 forced

Question **1** and question **8** are both part of a passive phrase. In question **1** 'be' tells you to look for a verb 3, and in question **8** 'are' does the same. In the box there are only four verbs to choose from.

See SKILLS FOCUS in this unit - *Gap-filling tasks*, page 74.

2   No word for anxiety

9   anxiety
10 learning to drive
11 because of a shared language,
    culture and experience of racism.
12 D
13 B
14 A
15 B

All *three* points are needed.

16 O
17 G
18 N
19 J
20 L
21 B
22 K
23 A
24 F

See SKILLS FOCUS in this unit - *Gap-filling tasks*, page 74.

Writing

Self assessment: Did you do the usual checks?
Did you use the reading passage for information? Did you answer the question properly, by *giving* information and then *asking* for more information?

Here is a model answer (although others, of course, are possible).

Dear Sir/Madam

I am writing to inform you about the loss of my passport and to request a new one. I lost it on 9th October, at Leeds bus station. My passport number is A4847009X. It was issued on 30th February 1987 and expires on 29th February 1997. I reported its loss to the police in Leeds immediately after the incident. The police reference number is CX241.

I would be grateful if you could tell me what documents I need to send you in order to be issued with a new passport. Do you require any passport photographs, and if so how many? How much will a new passport cost and in which currency would you like me to pay?

I apologise for any inconvenience caused and look forward to hearing from you.

Yours faithfully

B Biggins

BRIAN BIGGINS

See SKILLS FOCUS in this unit - *Writing a letter seeking information*, page 73.

Listening

1 D
2 A
3 D
4 C
5 Mark
6 Leigh-on-Sea
7 35211
8 Ricoh
9 4.55 pm
10 Will call back to collect.

Did you stop the tape as instructed, and study the pictures carefully? For question 1 you needed to count the number of figures *before* listening to the tape.

Speaking

Student A

Did you understand your role card? You wanted to ask as many questions as possible. Did you ask questions about all the things listed? How did you ask your first question? Was it like this?

'Excuse me. Could you tell me what time the trains go to Manchester?'

What about your next question? Do you think it is necessary to say 'Excuse me' again? And do you think an indirect question like the one above is necessary for your second question? Probably the best way to ask your second question is like this:

'What time do they arrive in Manchester?'

Your first question serves to get attention and to be polite, so an indirect question is appropriate. After that, direct, short questions are appropriate.

Student B

Did you have sufficient information to answer your partner's questions? Did you feel your partner's questions were appropriate? If not, why not?

Skills Focus
Writing a letter seeking information

You saw a possible answer to the writing task in this unit in the key on page 72.

1 Look at it again, and underline expressions which are only found in a letter.
   Example: *Dear Sir/Madam*

2 There are two main paragraphs. Which one *gives* information?
                                         asks for information?

Practice 1

Look at these two letters to a language school in Britain. Which is more appropriate? Why?

Letter A

Dear Sir/Madam

SUBJECT: Summer Language Course

With due respect I wish to request of you information regarding the language courses at your institution commencing in August. Would you therefore kindly inform me of the dates, cost, and facilities of the afore-mentioned courses?

Thanking you in advance, I remain

Faithfully yours

R B RYTIG

Letter B

Dear Sir/Madam

I am writing to request information about your summer language courses. I would be grateful if you could tell me the dates, facilities available, and how much they will cost. Thank you for your assistance.

I look forward to hearing from you.

Yours faithfully

B A WILBURY

Both are formal letters, and ask for the same information. **Letter A**, however, uses language which is more formal than is needed in English. **Letter B** is polite and appropriate; note that there is no need for a subject line as it is not a business letter, and the standard way of ending a formal letter: 'I look forward to hearing from you.', and 'Yours faithfully' (after Dear Sir/Madam). Don't forget to write 'Yours sincerely' if you wrote Dear (name) at the top.

Practice 2

Using the letter in the key and **Letter B** above, now write a letter to a language school in your area which runs the IELTS test, asking about registration, fees and dates.

Begin:

Dear Sir/Madam

Skills Focus
Gap-filling tasks

Both reading tasks in this unit required you to fill gaps in a text. You may find tasks of this type in your IELTS reading and listening papers; you may or may not be given words to choose from.

What do you think the missing word is in each of these sentences?

1 I went to the _____ because I had terrible toothache.

2 He _____ watching television when the bomb exploded.

3 I love ice-cream, but my husband _____ it.

How did you know what the missing word was? Like this?

GRAMMAR   LINKING WORD   VOCABULARY

1 I went to (the) dentist (because) I had terrible (toothache.)
   ⌐this indicates a   ⌐indicates a cause   ⌐You go to the dentist when
    noun to follow   (toothache) and a   you have toothache
                          result (➡ dentist)

All these – grammar, words linking parts of a sentence, and your knowledge of vocabulary – can help you to predict a missing word. Mark sentences **2** and **3** in the same way.

Practice I

Match each of the lettered gaps (**a-g**) in the passage below to one of the grammar labels on the right.

I've got _____**a**_____ brothers. Both of them are _____**b**__ than me, and both are very _____**c**_____. _____**d**__ I don't see them very often, we get on well. I'm hoping to _____**e**_____ one of them, John, in Delhi next month; he is a businessman, and is _____**f**_____ all over the world by his ____**g**____ .

Label	Letter
noun	_____
verb 1	_____
number	_____
adjective	_____
verb 3	_____
linking word	_____
comparative	_____

Which *other* words helped you to decide? For example, 'than' after the second gap suggested a comparative. Can you think of one word for each gap?

Practice 2

Below is a reading passage about population patterns in the United Kingdom.
There are ten gaps. Complete the table below it, which requires you to give a
grammar label, as in Practice 1, and a possible word to go in the gap.

Population:
The United Kingdom population ____1____ by 1.6 per cent between 1981 and 1989, with a 20 per cent growth in the number of ____2____ over 75 and a 19 per cent growth in children under 14.

The ____3____ growth was in East Anglia (8 per cent) and the South-west (6.4 per cent), with a fall of 1.6 per cent in the North, North-west and Scotland.

The North-west still ____4____ the highest population density, with 870 people per sq km and the least ____5____ population is in Scotland, with 66 per sq km.

Northern Ireland has the highest birth rate in the UK and the EC, with 16.5 ____6____ per 1000 population a year. The lowest birth rate is 12.5 per thousand in the South-east and Scotland, which also has ____7____ highest UK death rate of 12.8 per 1000.

The number of births outside marriage more than doubled ____8____ 1981 and 1988 to 26.6 per cent of all births. The highest rate in 1989 was 33.1 per cent in the North-west. In the North and North-west over 80 per cent of births to mothers under 20 were outside marriage, and even ____9____ Northern Ireland the figure was 73 per cent.

The highest concentration of ethnic minorities is in the South-east, with 8.2 ____10____ of the population, followed by the West Midlands with 7.1 per cent. The lowest is the North with 1.1 per cent.

Number	Label	Word	Number	Label	Word
1	verb 2	_____	6	_____	births
2	_____	_____	7	_____	_____
3	_____	_____	8	preposition	_____
4	_____	has	9	_____	_____
5	_____	_____	10	_____	_____

Practice 3

Remember, trying to predict the *type* of word in a gap helps just as much if the gap-fill task is a summary of a reading passage from which the missing words must be taken. Try **The British on holiday**.

Look at the reading passage about British social rules on the next page, and the summary of it on the right. For each gap in the summary, write ONE or TWO words in the space provided. THESE WORDS MUST BE TAKEN FROM THE READING PASSAGE.

The British on holiday

Holidays are a time when the unwritten rules and conventions of everyday life are widely breached, and other rules, recognisably those of 'being-on-holiday', come into force. Take clothing, for example. The middle-aged man dressed in shorts, sandals and a patterned shirt, open at the neck, with a straw hat on his head, is scarcely recognisable as the sober-suited professional commuter who travels into the office for the rest of the year. By wearing these clothes, he is telling the world, and himself, that he is on holiday, that many of his usual social obligations are suspended, and that he can behave in ways that he would not contemplate in the work setting, and which he assumes will not be witnessed by colleagues. An unwritten rule of holiday-making (and of works outings and office parties) is that indiscretions and excesses are not held against you in the work situation. Our man's children also know that he is operating with different rules from those of everyday life, especially those concerned with what counts as a waste of money.

Summary

When British people go on _____1_____ , normal social rules are _____2_____ and behaviour changes. For example, a _____3_____ is hardly _____4_____ when on holiday, wearing different clothes because he wants the _____5_____ to know he is on holiday. Now he is able to_____6_____ very differently from before, believing that his _____7_____ will not see him. Even his _____8_____ understand that he is permitted to behave differently at this time.

Your answers

1 _____   5 _____

2 _____   6 _____

3 _____   7 _____

4 _____   8 _____

HEALTH

Reading   *You are advised to spend about 10 minutes on questions 1-11.*

Part 1 Selenium's role in thyroid found

Questions 1-8

The diagrams below illustrate Reading Passage 1, **Selenium's role in thyroid found**. Complete the diagram by finding the correct word(s) FROM THE TEXT to fill in each numbered space.

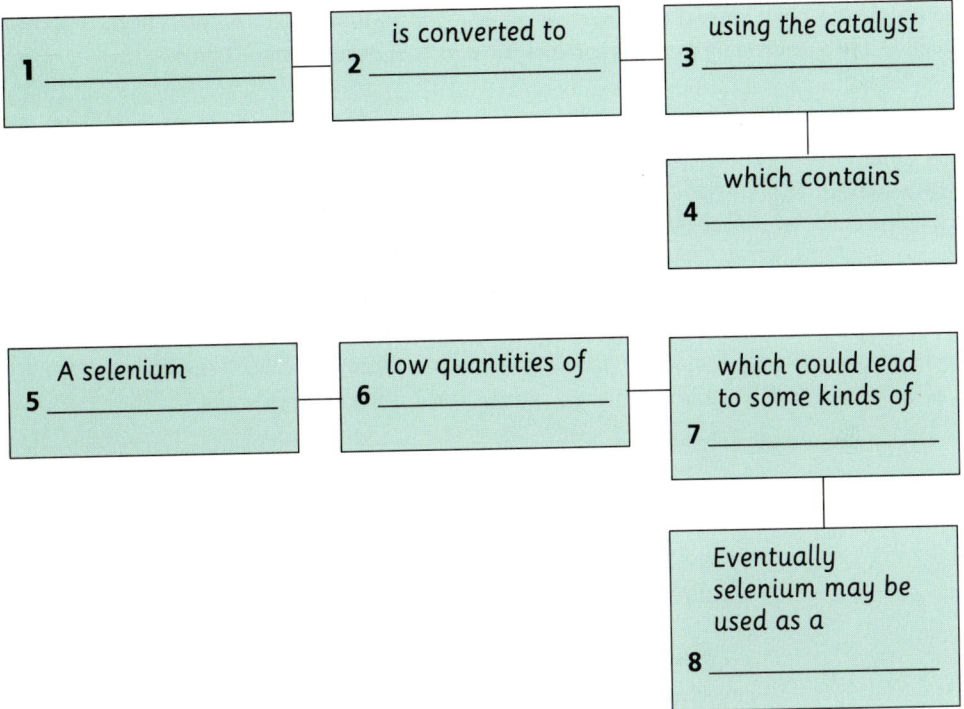

Reading Passage 1

Selenium's role in thyroid found

1 Scientists in West Germany have found that selenium is an essential component of an enzyme in the thyroid gland. The discovery indicates that selenium deficiency may play a role in certain diseases of metabolism, as iodine does. Eventually, selenium may be used to treat certain thyroid ailments.

2 Researchers found that selenium is part of the enzyme deiodinase, which catalyses the production of hormones in the thyroid gland. Specifically, deiodinase catalyses the production of triiothyronin (T3) from thyroxin (T4). In embryos, T3 regulates cell differentiation – the way in which the cells take up specialist functions. In adults, it increases the rate of most metabolic functions.

3 The existence of the enzyme was already known but it was not known that selenium was part of the functional group. Now it is known that in cases where there is a selenium deficiency, there will not be enough of the enzyme present. Without selenium, it is impossible to make T3.

4 Researchers have been investigating selenium's role in the body since 1957. The element is toxic in high doses. More research is being done to try to discover the health effects of decreases in T3 production.

5 One of the things that researchers already know is that in areas of the world where there is little or no selenium in the environment, certain thyroid diseases are more common. These include diseases such as Keshan disease, or endemic cardiomyopathy. People suffering from this disease were fed dietary supplements of sodium selenite – a treatment which has practically eradicated the disease.

6 But despite the successful clinical applications of selenium, some researchers are sceptical about using selenium supplements for the general population. There have been controversial claims that it helps against cancer, provides protection from radiation, and even AIDS. But there is little proof of this. Most researchers believe that if you have got enough selenium already, more won't help, and too much will have a toxic effect.

Questions 9-11

Look at the reading passage, **Selenium's role in thyroid found,** and answer the following questions.

Choose which of the alternatives **A,B,C** or **D** is the correct answer and put the appropriate letter in the space provided.

Your answers

9 What is the conclusion of paragraph 1?

   A Selenium has medical potential.
   B Selenium deficiency causes certain diseases.
   C Selenium is an essential component of thyroid enzyme.
   D Selenium acts in the same way as iodine.

   9 _____

10 T3 is important in embryos because:

   A of the way the cells take different functions.
   B it increases the rate of metabolic functions.
   C it acts as a regulator of the differentiation of cells.
   D it produces the enzyme deiodinase.

   10 _____

11 Although selenium is an essential element in a healthy adult:

    A it can cause thyroid diseases.
    B too much of the substance may have a toxic effect.
    C it is dangerous for embryos.
    D a deficiency has no effect upon health.   11 _____

Part 2 Nicotine on the brain

You are advised to spend about 20 minutes on questions 12-25.

Questions 12-14

The reading passage, **Nicotine on the brain,** identifies four addictive effects of nicotine. From the following list decide which are the four effects and write the letter in the space provided. The first one has been done as an example.

Example: _____E_____

12 _____

13 _____

14 _____

A	The taste and smell of the smoke
B	Withdrawal symptoms
C	Vomiting
D	Experiencing a 'high' after smoking
E	Positive reinforcement
F	Tolerance to nicotine's behavioural effects
G	Improvement in aspects of learning
H	Dementia
I	A change in behaviour corresponding to a change in quantity of nicotine

Questions 15-17

Each of the following questions can be answered with a phrase in the list **A-F** in the box. Decide which phrase answers each question and write the letter in the space provided.

Reading Passage 2 gives three reasons why tobacco is unusual amongst addictive drugs. What are they?

Your answers

15 Reason 1

16 Reason 2

17 Reason 3

15 _____

16 _____

17 _____

A	Some effects are useful	D	It is composed of many chemicals
B	It is rewarding	E	Withdrawal effects are not severe
C	There is no 'high' like heroin	F	It affects behaviour

Reading Passage 2

Nicotine on the brain

Why do people inhale the smoke of the burning dried leaves of the tobacco plant despite numerous warnings from experts that it may kill them? The answer seems to be, in part, that inhaling tobacco smoke is the fastest and most efficient way yet discovered to get nicotine into the human brain – and that nicotine is addictive. Scientists have now established that nicotine promotes addictive behaviour just as effectively as drugs traditionally considered to be addictive and they have begun to discover how it does so.

Although tobacco smoke is a complex mixture of thousands of different chemicals, it is nicotine that produces most of the immediate effects of smoking on the body, and the addictive effects on brain and behaviour. But it is substances in the smoke called 'tar' that are mainly responsible for diseases such as lung cancer. So, the effects that smokers seek may be separable from those that do the physical damage. We may be able to devise strategies to limit the damage caused by smoking, and to help people to quit.

But why do scientists now believe that nicotine is addictive? In the early 1960s, most experts believed that smoking was a psychologically-based habit that people indulged in to experience the taste and smell of the smoke, to see the pretty patterns of the smoke-rings, and to gain oral satisfaction in the psychoanalytic sense.

By the late 1970s, psychopharmacologists such as Steven Goldberg and Roger Spealman, at Harvard University in Massachusetts, had demonstrated that solutions of pure nicotine could serve as a reward – a so-called positive reinforcer, in the language of behavioural psychology. This simply means that people can learn or become 'conditioned' to find nicotine rewarding, and so continue to seek it out. Experiments also showed that people altered their smoking behaviour when researchers altered the amount of nicotine delivered by their cigarettes, or gave them nicotine-like or nicotine-blocking drugs. Animals can readily detect the characteristic subjective effects of nicotine and can distinguish these from the effects of other drugs.

Other studies showed that tolerance developed to some, but not all, of nicotine's effects on behaviour. For example, doses of nicotine that make non-smokers vomit fail to do so in regular smokers. Classical addictive drugs such as heroin also produce tolerance. Such tolerance can persist for several months after exposure to nicotine ends, and may be why people who have given up smoking are likely to relapse. Further evidence that nicotine is addictive is the fact that smokers experience withdrawal symptoms when they give up.

In 1980 the evidence was so compelling that few researchers in the field questioned the addictive nature of tobacco. But doctors and the public at large have been slow to accept this finding because heroin tends to be seen as a model for all addictions. Heroin addicts experience an immediate 'high' after taking the drug and suffer severe withdrawal symptoms if they stop taking it. People assumed that the different effects of nicotine meant that it was not really addictive. Tobacco is also unusual among abused substances in that users may find some of the short-term psychological effects useful, in altering mood or attention, say. Moreover, the symptoms of withdrawal from tobacco are quite different from, and less severe than, withdrawal from opiates. Yet addiction to drugs should not be defined merely by withdrawal reactions. Central to all addiction, whether to a stimulant, a tranquilliser, alcohol or nicotine, is the way the drug itself reinforces behaviour. That is, people learn to find its use rewarding. The reduction of withdrawal symptoms is one mechanism of reinforcement, but it is not the only one, even for opiates. If the ability to produce striking withdrawal syndrome is the main criterion, cocaine as well as nicotine would have to be considered non-addictive. It is the strength, not the nature, of the reinforcing effect that determines addictiveness.

All the same, it is important to understand the nature of the positive reinforcing effect of nicotine that can keep people smoking. Several ideas are currently under discussion. Jack Henningfield of the Addiction Research Center in Baltimore, Maryland, has shown that nicotine can produce a state of euphoria, a feeling of well-being that has no basis in reality, which resembles the effects of classical addictive drugs. But the intensity of this effect is probably not sufficient to explain why smoking is so reinforcing.

Other scientists believe that nicotine can enhance certain psychological functions in ways that are actually important and useful for smokers. David Warburton of the University of Reading suggests that nicotine can improve concentration and enhance accuracy during the performance of boring tasks that require sustained attention over long periods of time. There is also evidence that nicotine may improve aspects of learning and memory and the ability to process information rapidly. Here, we need further research to distinguish more rigorously between real benefits due to nicotine and the mere alleviation of declines in performance caused by nicotine's withdrawal. Nevertheless, the observations have encouraged attempts to use nicotine to overcome some of the problems in learning and memory in dementias such as Alzheimer's disease.

Another source of reinforcement that is widely discussed today is more straightforward: people may continue to smoke merely to prevent nicotine withdrawal syndrome.

So researchers do not yet fully understand why using nicotine is positively reinforcing, although all these different effects may play a role. Factors that may be most important for one person may not be very significant for others. Yet there may still be a common brain mechanism that ultimately converts the different aspects of nicotine's positive reinforcing effect into drug-seeking behaviour, and much current research aims to identify this elusive central mechanism.

Questions 18-25

The following are statements about smoking.

If a statement is supported in Reading Passage 2, circle **A**. If it is rejected, circle **B**, and if it is not discussed, circle **C**.

	Supported in the text	Rejected in the text	Not discussed in the text
Example: Smoking is one of the fastest ways of getting nicotine to the brain.	(A)	B	C
18 Nicotine is responsible for the behavioural effects of smoking.	A	B	C
19 Nicotine is responsible for diseases such as lung cancer.	A	B	C
20 Smoking is a psychologically-based habit.	A	B	C
21 Nicotine does not have any similar properties to classical addictive drugs.	A	B	C
22 Tobacco is an abused substance.	A	B	C
23 A good way of defining addiction is by withdrawal symptoms.	A	B	C
24 People keep smoking because of pressure from society.	A	B	C
25 Nicotine has no positive effects.	A	B	C

W r i t i n g *You should spend no more than 15 minutes on this task.*

Smoking is a major killer in our societies today. The reasons are known and death is easily avoided.

TASK **As a class assignment you have been asked to do the following task:**

Write a short paragraph describing the effects of smoking upon health and the benefits gained from stopping.

You may use your own knowledge and experience in addition to the notes provided.

Your description should be:

1 relevant to the task and
2 well organised.

You should write at least 100 words.

```
                    SMOKING

   Possible diseases        Life Expectancy

       Bronchitis            People killed by
      Heart Disease        smoking - average loss
        Cancer               - 10 to 15 years


    Pregnancy risk          Stopping smoking

      Miscarriage           Nearly all risks of
    Premature Birth         death or disability
                              are avoided
```

Listening

Section 1 Questions 1-8

Circle **T** for TRUE and **F** for FALSE.

		True	False
1	There are eight beds in the ward.	T	F
2	The hospital supplies clean clothes for patients.	T	F
3	You can only have two visitors per day.	T	F
4	The patient has breakfast at 8.00 am at home.	T	F
5	The hospital allows smoking in certain places.	T	F
6	The hospital gives patients a bill for any phone calls.	T	F
7	Too many friends and relatives telephone the hospital each day.	T	F
8	Patients can listen to the hospital radio without disturbing the other patients.	T	F

Section 2 Questions 9-16

Fill in the gaps in the report on the news item by writing in the missing words in the column to the right of the passage.

Your answers

In today's programme Janet Newman talks about the ___9___ of Henton Hospital. It was built in 1924 with ___10___ beds. Now the old building houses ___11___ A to H, and the physiotherapy department. In the late fifties the hospital was extended to 800 beds. It is now a ___12___ hospital, and is famous for its open heart surgery. Several famous ___13___ have come to the hospital including the Queen. The ___14___ , Johnny Brown, has raised a lot of money, which helped to buy the body scanner last ___15___ .The hospital radio began ___16___ in 1972.

9 _____

10 _____

11 _____

12 _____

13 _____

14 _____

15 _____

16 _____

Speaking

Work with a partner. One of you look at **Role Card A**, and the other at **Role Card B.**

Role Card A

Imagine you are a patient entering hospital. Speak to the nurse (Student B) and find out as much as possible about hospital rules.

SOME THINGS TO FIND OUT:

- things to bring with you
- meal times
- visitors
- telephone calls
- times of getting up / going to bed
- entertainment (books, radio, TV)
- smoking

Role Card B

Imagine you are a nurse. Answer the questions from your new patient (Student A) with the help of the information below.

HOSPITAL RULES

Things to bring
Several sets clean night clothes
Toothbrush
Books to read

Meals
Breakfast 6.15 am
Morning Coffee 9.45 am
Lunch 12 noon
Afternoon Tea 3.15 pm
Dinner 5.45 pm

Phone calls
Out-going: payphone (change required) brought to your bed.
Incoming: relatives should call the Duty Sister (ext. 405)

Visitors
Maximum 2 at any one time
Visiting hours: 11-12 am
                            3.30-5 pm

Bed-time
Evening lights out: 9.30 pm
Morning Alarm: 5.45 am

Other information
No smoking in wards –
please use designated lounges
Hospital Radio broadcasts
2-7 pm
Television: in TV lounge
Questions or complaints
should be addressed to the
Ward Sister

Key and feedback

Reading

Part 1 Selenium's role in thyroid found

1 Thyroxin/ T4
2 Triiothyronin/ T3
3 deiodinase
4 selenium

5 deficiency
6 T3/triiothyronin enzyme
7 thyroid diseases
8 treatment

This is a tricky kind of question because the information in the text is in a different order from the flow diagram. The way to approach this kind of question is to read the appropriate paragraph(s) carefully first. You also need to recognise word families, so that where the flow diagram uses the **noun** catalyst, the text uses the **verb** catalyses, and you know that the subject of the verb is the **catalyst**.

9 A
10 C
11 B

The *conclusion* is the writer's opinion of the use of this discovery.

Part 2 Nicotine on the brain
in any order:
12 I
13 F
14 B
in any order:
15 C
16 A
17 E

These answers are found in paragraph 6. The sentence beginning 'Tobacco is also unusual...' The 'also' tells you to look *back* for one point and then forward for the rest.

18 A
19 B
20 B
21 B
22 A
23 B
24 C
25 B

Notice that these questions are not quite the same as TRUE, FALSE and NOT GIVEN in Unit 1.

Writing

Did you follow the instructions and write a single paragraph? The paragraph could have been organised into five parts (parts, NOT paragraphs), starting with a short sentence about smoking, for example:

Many people in the world today smoke despite knowing the dangers and risks it carries.

The next part should go on to describe possible diseases caused by smoking, followed by a description of risks to pregnant women. Next a sentence or two about the life expectancy, and how it is reduced by 10 to 15 years for smokers. Finally, you could finish your task with a description of the effects of stopping smoking.

Listening

Section 1
  1 T
  2 F
  3 F
  4 F
  5 T
  6 F
  7 T
  8 T

Section 2
  9 history
10 200
11 wards
12 teaching
13 visitors
14 comedian
15 month
16 broadcasting

Speaking

Student A

In this speaking task you had to make questions to find out some information. Did your first question sound like this?

   'Can you tell me what things I need to bring with me when I come to hospital?'

This is a nice, polite way to start your questions. The next question, however, doesn't need to be an indirect question. It sounds better as a direct one:

   'What time are the meals?'

It is also better if you can vary the question types, so your next question could begin with:

   'What about...'

For more practice with asking questions see SKILLS FOCUS in Unit 5 - *Speaking: Asking questions*, page 60.

Intonation is also very important in order to sound polite. See SKILLS FOCUS in this unit - *Speaking: Intonation in questions*, page 89.

Student B

Did you have sufficient information to answer your partner's questions? What kind of questions did your partner ask? Were they appropriate and polite all the time? If not, *why not?* Think about *how* your partner asked the questions, as well as *what they asked*. The way we ask is as important as *what* we ask. See SKILLS FOCUS in this unit - *Speaking: Intonation in questions*, page 89.

Skills Focus
Reading - Guessing meaning from context

Was there any vocabulary in the reading passage in this unit that you could not understand? Did you feel you *needed* to understand it? If you could answer the questions successfully anyway, you probably either:

1) did not need to understand the vocabulary

or

2) *guessed* the meaning of the vocabulary.

A What helps you to guess the meaning of unknown words? Let's look at two examples from Reading Passage 1.

1 Imagine you are having difficulty with the word 'deficiency' from the paragraph below. Underline the key words in the paragraph.

Scientists in West Germany have found that selenium is an essential component of an enzyme in the thyroid gland. The discovery indicates that selenium **deficiency** may play a role in certain diseases of metabolism, as iodine does. Eventually, selenium may be used to treat certain thyroid ailments.

Compare your key words with this list:

Sentence 1: SELENIUM / ESSENTIAL / THYROID GLAND

Sentence 2: SELENIUM / **DEFICIENCY** / DISEASES

Sentence 3: SELENIUM / TREAT / THYROID AILMENTS

If selenium is *essential* in the thyroid gland, what could cause disease? Probably too much or too little of it. 'Deficiency' could mean either of these. However, sentence 3 tells us that selenium can be given as a treatment, which suggests it is useful; 'too little' selenium is therefore a more likely problem than 'too much'. Following this logic, deficiency means 'too little'.

2 Another example: 'sceptical' this time.

But despite the successful clinical applications of selenium, some researchers are **sceptical** about using selenium supplements for the general population.

'Despite' + something positive ('successful clinical applications') is always followed by something negative. Which of the following, do you think, is the best synonym for 'sceptical' in this context?

HAPPY / DOUBTFUL / OPPOSED / EXCITED

In both of these examples, the **context,** that is, the language around the unknown word, helped to establish the meaning. **Context is often the best dictionary!**

87

B Now use the context of the underlined words in the following sentences to try and work out their meaning. Choose the best option, **a**, **b** or **c**.

1

> Researchers in Cambridge are in a <u>quandary</u> over finances following the death of eminent cancer researcher A P Simmons. Should the £1 million he left be spent on a museum, as he wished, or on continuing the work on cancer he himself started?

Quandary:
    a argument about a decision
    b problem to which there is no possible answer
    c state of doubt about a decision

2

> The leader of the opposition voiced the discontent of many when he <u>harangued</u> the Prime Minister over the government's decision to increase taxes.

Harangued:
    a spoke angrily to
    b tried to persuade
    c annoyed

3

> Researchers have discovered that many patients with bad <u>scalds</u> are almost completely unable to remember the actual moment when the boiling liquid hit their skin.

Scalds:
    a injuries to the brain affecting memory
    b injuries caused by boiling liquid or steam
    c injuries to the skin

4

> Look around you in any big city, and you will see buildings coated with the <u>grime</u> left behind by air pollution, darkening every wall and leaving you with dirty fingers if you are unlucky enough to touch it.

Grime:
    a stone or concrete
    b dirt on a surface
    c poor quality paint

5

> After reading a book which you feel is important for your particular field of studies, it is always worth making a brief <u>synopsis</u> enabling you to refer back quickly and aiding your memory at a later date.

Synopsis:
    a word for word copy
    b criticism
    c summary of the main points

Skills Focus
Speaking - Intonation in questions

In Unit 5, SKILLS FOCUS - *Asking questions*, page 60, you looked at how to form polite and varied questions.
Now we need to think about *how* to say them.

Listen to the tape. You will hear five questions. Decide if the questions sound polite or not, and tick or cross the number accordingly.

1 _____   2 _____   3 _____   4 _____   5 _____

What helped you to decide – the words used, or the way the speaker said the questions?

The way we speak (how our voice goes up and down, or *intonation*) is often more important than the words or structures we use. Intonation makes a question more effective. Listen to six more questions on the tape, listed below. Does the voice go up ⤴ or down ⤵ ? We've marked the first one for you.

1 Are you married?

2 Do you like mangoes?

3 Where are you from?

4 How long have you been here?

5 Could you tell me your name, please?

6 Would you mind opening the window?

What rules can you make about the intonation of Yes / No questions (**1** and **2** above), Wh-questions (**3** and **4**) and indirect questions (**5** and **6**)?

Notice that all types start very high but end in different ways.
⬆ ⬆ ⬆

Yes / No questions start high, and end with a slight fall and then a rise:

Are you English?

Wh-questions start high, and fall:

Where's the bank?

Indirect questions start high, then fall, but often end on a 'polite' rise, sometimes on the word 'please':

Could you tell me the time, please?

Practice 1

Work with a partner. Look back at the list of nine questions at the start of SKILLS FOCUS - *Asking questions*, page 60, in Unit 5. Identify the kind of question each one is: (Yes / No, Wh- or indirect), and try saying them using the patterns above. Remember to start high! Listen to each other and decide if you sound polite, or record yourself and listen to your own intonation.

Practice 2

Work in threes. The Speaking tasks in Units 2, 5, 6 and 7 require you to ask questions. Choose one of these tasks. Two of you take the A and B roles, while the third person listens carefully to check that you are still using good intonation during a conversation.

EDUCATION

▶ **R e a d i n g** *You are advised to spend about 15 minutes on questions 1-11 which refer to Reading Passage 1.*

Questions 1-5

Reading passage 1, **Education for the rural disadvantaged**, has six paragraphs. For each paragraph, choose the best heading from the list **A-I** in the box below, and write the letter in the space provided. There are more headings than you need. The first one has been done as an example.

> A Insufficient access to education
> B Rural poverty
> C Rural populations of developing countries
> D Realistic aims
> E Education in developing countries
> F Rural primary education for the few
> G Educational ideals
> H Financing education
> I A view of the future

Example : Paragraph 1 ____C____
1 Paragraph 2 _____
2 Paragraph 3 _____
3 Paragraph 4 _____
4 Paragraph 5 _____
5 Paragraph 6 _____

Reading Passage 1

Education for the rural disadvantaged

1 The vast majority of people in the developing countries live in rural areas, on farms, in villages or in rural market towns. In some countries, such as Rwanda, Burkina Faso and Malawi more than 90 percent of the total population lives in the rural areas.

2 The projections are that the rural populations of the less-developed countries will increase substantially in the decades to come. The UN predicts these will increase from 1.9 billion in 1970 to 2.6 billion by 1990. Thailand's rural population alone will increase from 30.6 million in 1970 to 570 million by the year 2000. Furthermore, because of high birth rates and declining infant mortality rates, more than half of the rural population of developing countries is under 20 years of age. This raises serious implications for education.

3 The main purpose of education is to provide *everybody* (not only those in urban areas) with relevant knowledge, skills, attitudes and ideas which will enable them to lead more fulfilling, productive and satisfying lives. To assert that everyone has a 'right' to education has little practical meaning unless this

'right' is translated into terms of some 'minimum package' of attitudes, knowledge and skills for *all* people in a given society. To do otherwise is to create a privileged class at the expense of everyone else. Vague objectives such as 'giving every child a good basic education' (often defined as four to six or more years of formal schooling) are meaningless when huge sections of the population are getting little or no education at all.

4   People in rural areas suffer from inadequate educational facilities and opportunities. In most rural areas in developing countries the out-of-school group constitutes a vast majority of the whole population from, say, 10 to 20 years old. For all practical purposes, they are beyond the reach of formal education. But no section of the community should be shortchanged by its educational system.

5   Where there are rural primary schools they benefit far fewer rural young people than educational statistics often imply. Primary schools, instead of being the great equalisers of educational opportunity they were meant to be, are the great discriminators. In the rural areas they equip only a small minority of the young for effective and satisfying adulthood. The great majority of rural youngsters are destined to live out the all-too-familiar grind of ignorance and poverty.

6   This vicious circle has to be broken; the goal must be to provide everybody with basic knowledge and skills. Rather than attempt to enrol every child for a seven or-eight-year cycle of primary schooling, which is not financially feasible anyway for many countries for many years to come, the strategy should be a shorter four to five-year primary cycle to provide every child with the minimum educational needs – literacy, numeracy, health education and those technical and entrepreneurial skills needed to make a decent living. This primary education should be geared for the large majority who will not continue their studies beyond this stage, who will enter straight into productive life.

Questions 6-11

Decide whether the author of Reading Passage 1 has a positive or negative attitude to the statements below, or whether it is impossible to tell what his attitude is. Write **+** if the author has a positive attitude, **–** if negative, or IT if it is impossible to tell, in the space provided. The first one has been done as an example.

	Your answers
Example: Most rural 10 - 20 year olds are beyond the reach of formal education.	—
6 Over half the rural population in developing countries is under 20.	_____
7 The aim of education is to equip everybody for effective and satisfying adulthood.	_____
8 Education can create a privileged class.	_____
9 Every rural child should be enrolled in a 7 or 8 year cycle of primary schooling.	_____
10 Every rural child should be enrolled in a 4 or 5 year cycle of primary schooling.	_____
11 Many rural children start work immediately after primary school.	_____

Read the passage below, and answer questions 12-21 which follow.
You should spend about 15 minutes on questions 12-21.

Reading Passage 2

Come to a full stop
The Perils of Punctuation

Punctuation makes the written language intelligible. It does the job, on the page, of the changes of pitch, pace and rhythm which make it possible to understand speech. Unsurprisingly, therefore, a requirement for some knowledge of how to punctuate makes an early appearance in an English curriculum.

The trouble is, that necessary though punctuation is, the task of teaching it to adults and children is considerably more challenging than it might appear. To believe, for example, that it is possible to instruct children about writing in sentences by telling them about full stops and capital letters is to court frustration and failure. The notion of the sentence as a statement – a free-standing chunk of information – is something that children come to gradually. Nor, interestingly, do they come first to short sentences and then proceed to longer ones. For a child, the piece of information which 'free-stands' in the head may be a whole description or section of narrative. She may be reading three-word sentences in her reading book, but her own writing will be in chunks of up to a page.

Gradually, as written work grows longer and more complicated, so the perception of the shorter sentence increases. Good teachers will, in their teaching of early writing, watch for the child's ability to compose in sentences, and then point out how the use of punctuation will define them more clearly.

So where, in all this, comes the mechanical definition of a sentence – that it needs a verb, for example? The pragmatic answer, I suspect, is that it comes nowhere at all. Adult writers do not, on the whole, look back at their sentences to make sure they contain verbs. We all, surely, feel our sentences intuitively. Most of the time, to be sure, they will contain verbs. Occasionally, though, they may not – and where's the harm? What is certain is that you cannot possibly use the grammatical rule as a tool with which to teach a seven-year-old about sentence-writing. The child can be nudged and helped towards writing in sentences, but on the whole she will not do it until she is ready.

The point is that punctuation is an aid which the writer brings into play to illuminate an already formed idea. Before you can learn the punctuation, you have to know what you want to punctuate. A child's readiness to take teaching about punctuation can best be judged by her ability to use the constructions for which the punctuation is needed. Thus you teach capital letters, full stops, question marks and exclamation marks to a child who is already writing sentences, questions and exclamations. Similarly, you teach direct speech punctuation to a child who is already writing dialogue. The development of the child's writing will always be a step ahead of the punctuation, and to reverse the process in response, say, to the short-term demands of a curriculum, is to put later progress at risk.

This, incidentally, makes assessment notoriously difficult. How do you compare the writing of a child who writes in correctly punctuated simple sentences with that of the child who writes good, but unpunctuated, dialogue?

Finally, what about the most misused device in the English language – the apostrophe? The problem which teachers have here is that we are living in the midst of change. The conventions we were all taught are not really difficult, but they do call for a fairly sophisticated level of conceptual understanding. There are traps, too, lurking within such distinctions as that between 'it's' and 'its', and even the most competent of writers is likely to be floored occasionally by words which end with 's' and are not plurals. How confidently would you render, 'The strings of the double bass', in apostrophised form, for example?

Questions 12 and 13

Using Reading Passage 2, fill in the spaces in the table below.

Punctuation	is equivalent to	**12** _____
13 _____		a statement or chunk of information

Questions 14 - 16

Choose ONE or TWO words from the text to fill in each gap in the statements.

14 Children slowly acquire the _____ that information exists in individual chunks, or sentences.

15 A good way for teachers to help their students is by showing them how punctuation aids meaning at a time when the child shows the _____ write sentences.

16 The apostrophe causes many difficulties and is frequently _____.

Questions 17 and 18

Decide which option, **A, B, C** or **D** is best and write the letter in the space provided.

17 The author believes that sentences which do not contain a verb are:

    A carelessly written sentences.
    B useful in teaching punctuation.
    C not incorrect sentences.
    D based on intuition rather than grammar.

          Your answer _____

18 According to the text, punctuation is naturally used when:

    A a writer already knows what she/he means to say.
    B a writer needs an aid.
    C long or complex sentences are written.
    D writing sentences, questions and exclamations.

          Your answer _____

19 What, according to the passage, might make a teacher teach punctuation before constructions?

          Your answer _____

Questions 20 and 21

Write down two factors which, according to the passage, make the apostrophe a problem for writers.

20 _____

21 _____

W r i t i n g   *You should spend no more than 30 minutes on this task.*

Reading Passage 1 considered education for rural people in developing countries.

TASK **Write an essay for a university teacher on the following topic:**

Education is the single most important factor in the development of a developing country.

You should make sure that your essay is well-organised, and expresses your own opinions as well as giving relevant examples.

You should write at least 150 words.

Listening

Section 1
Questions 1-4

Listen to two students talking about a diploma course, and put ticks in the correct places in the table. You can use ONE or TWO ticks for each question. The first one has been done for you as an example.

Components of the diploma		Interesting	Easy	Moderate	Difficult
Orientation Course **Example:**			✓		
Written Component	1				
Practical Component	2				
Practical Exams	3				
Written Exams	4				

Section 2
Questions 5-13

Listen to the interview about school days, and answer questions 5-13 by writing a word or short phrase.

5   What type of school did Diana go to? _____

6   How many pupils were there in each class? _____

7   Give THREE subjects that were compulsory. _____

8   What is the name of the type of exams the interviewer asks about? _____

9   What was the maximum number of exams that could be taken? _____

10 How did the pupils treat teachers with poor discipline? _____

11 Who had to wear uniforms? _____

12 What new development regarding uniform does Diana mention? _____

13 When did Diana have exams? _____

Speaking

An IELTS maze

If you don't already know, use a dictionary or ask your teacher to find out what a 'maze' is.

Think about the evening before your IELTS test. What are you planning to do that evening? Discuss your plans with a partner. Then you can enter the maze. The first card is below. You will have to read some information, then make a decision with your partner(s). If you are in a class, your teacher will give you another card with the number of your choice. If you are working alone, cut up the cards on pages 99-103, turn them face down, and turn up the numbers of your choice as you choose them. See how long it takes you to get out of the maze successfully...

Number 1

Your IELTS test is tomorrow morning at 9.00am. You know you have not done enough work.
Do you:

- Stay up all night working?   Go to **16**
- Spend all night copying cards
  to try to take into the exam
  with you?   Go to **11**
- Spend the evening relaxing?   Go to **3**

After the maze -

- What good decisions did you make?
- What poor decisions did you make?
- What do you now intend to do the evening before your IELTS test?

Number 2

Your friend leaves miserably, and you feel horribly guilty. Do you:

- Go out and find him/her?   Go to **14**
- Go back to bed and try to sleep?   Go to **9**

Number 3

You try to relax but find it impossible.
Do you:

- Do a little work on some grammar? Go to **19**
- Go to visit some friends who
  live nearby?   Go to **5**
- Decide to stay up all night
  after all?   Go to **16**

Number 4

You telephone your teacher at 11.00 at night. He is furious and tells you to go back to bed.

Go back to **1**

Number 5

You go to your friend's house, but after an hour you begin to worry again.
Do you:

- Go home and do a little work? Go to **19**
- Go home and watch television? Go to **8**
- Stay with your friends to be polite? Go to **6**

Number 6

You stay with your friends another hour and find yourself irritable and rude, so you finally decide to leave them and go home.

Go to **3**

Number 7

Your friend comes in, but soon you realise he/she is making you panic.
Do you:

- Tell him/her to leave? Go to **2**
- Tell him/her that he/she can stay and watch TV, but you are going to bed whether he/she likes it or not! Go to **17**

Number 8

You watch a TV programme about the psychological effects of taking exams! This does not help to relax you so you switch it off.

Go to **3**

Number 9

You fall asleep. Your alarm wakes you; it is time for the exam. You have had a good night's sleep. Good luck! You are out of the maze.

Number 10

You are reading and begin to get sleepy when there's a knock at the door. Do you:

- Ignore it and try to go to sleep? Go to **18**
- Get up and answer it? Go to **13**

Number 11

You start copying cards but after a while you realise it's an impossible task and have a look at some vocabulary instead.

Go to **15**

Number 12

You realise you're panicking and not getting anywhere. Do you:

● Telephone your teacher for advice? Go to **4**
● Decide to visit your friends? Go to **5**
● Abandon grammar and do a little
  vocabulary? Go to **15**

Number 13

You get up and answer the door to find a classmate panicking about the exam. Do you:

● Invite him/her in and try to
  relax him/her? Go to **7**
● Suggest he/she tries to relax,
  but send him/her home anyway? Go to **2**

Number 14

You start wandering the streets, realise it's a bad idea, so you go back home. Do you:

● Switch on the TV? Go to **8**
● Start reading a book? Go to **10**

Number 15

You spend an hour on vocabulary and then go to bed but you are too nervous to sleep. Do you:

● Stay in bed, trying to sleep? Go to **17**
● Turn on the light and read a
  grammar book again? Go to **12**
● Turn on the light and read
  a novel? Go to **10**

Number 16

You stay up all night swotting but get more and more confused. Do you:

● Continue reading your favourite
  grammar book? Go to **19**
● Start reading a class reader? Go to **10**
● Telephone your teacher for
  advice? Go to **4**

Number 17

After a couple of hours of tossing and turning and failing to sleep, you get up.

Go to **3**

Number 18

The caller continues to knock on the door. Do you:

● Continue to ignore it and wait
  for the person to go away? Go to **17**
● Get up and answer the door? Go to **13**

Number 19

While doing some work you decide you don't understand the present perfect. Do you:

● Try not to worry, and check some
  vocabulary instead? Go to **15**
● Try to contact your teacher? Go to **4**
● Read some pages of grammar
  notes again? Go to **12**

Key and feedback

Reading

1   Education for the rural disadvantaged

1 I
2 G
3 A
4 F
5 D

6 IT
7 +
8 –
9 –
10 +
11 IT

These questions asked you to distinguish between *fact* and the writer's *opinion*. Questions **6** and **11** are both factual statements; we cannot tell the author's opinion.

2   Come to a full stop

12   pitch, pace, rhythm in speech
13   (the) sentence

14   notion
15   ability to
16   misused

Notice the need for *two* words in question 15 to make grammatical sense.

17 C
18 A

19   (demands of a) curriculum

See the last line, fifth paragraph.

20 and 21 (in either order) distinction
        between 'it's'and 'its'
        words ending in 's' which are not plurals

Writing

Did you agree with the essay title or disagree? Or did you try to see *both* points of view? See the SKILLS FOCUS in this unit - *Writing an argument*, page 107.

Listening

Components of the diploma		Interesting	Easy	Moderate	Difficult
Orientation Course **Example:**			✓		
Written Component	1	✓		✓	
Practical Component	2	✓		✓	
Practical Exams	3				✓
Written Exams	4			✓	

5 Grammar
6 40
7 Any THREE from:
   English/maths/geography/history/sport
8 0 levels
9 9
10 took advantage (of them)
11 1st to 5th years
12 allowed trousers in winter
13 end of every term

Speaking

How long did it take you to get out of the 'maze'? What were your best decisions? And your worst? What lessons did you learn about what to do the night before your IELTS test...?

Skills Focus
Writing an argument

In this unit you had to write an essay on the following topic:

Education is the single most important factor in the development of a developing country.

Did you spend a few minutes *planning* the essay? How did you *organise* your answer? Did you achieve a *balance* of agreement and disagreement?

A good answer might be organised as follows:

Paragraph 1:   (FOR) *Why education is the most important factor*
⬇
Paragraph 2:   (AGAINST) *Why education is **not** the most important factor*
⬇
Paragraph 3:   (CONCLUSION) *My opinion*

Notice that an introduction is not really necessary in an essay of this length: perhaps just one or two lines.

Practice 1 Planning

A   Here is one writer's plan for paragraphs 1 and 2 of the essay above. Some of his arguments have been placed in the wrong column. Which ones? Draw an arrow (➡) to show where they should be, or tick (✓) them if they are in the right place.

Why education is the most important factor	Why education is not the most important factor
• Education provides basis for other skills **(Example: ✓)** • Health is more important than education • Literacy improves working person's capability • Expensive and without immediate financial return • Creates self/national respect	• Economic development is important, and may only need unskilled workers • Education provides basis for healthy population • Difficult to find enough trained teachers

Can you add any points to the columns?

B   Now write your own plan for this essay title. What could your two columns be?

Children should never be educated at home by their parents.

Practice 2 Writing the essay

A   Write (a) next to the expressions in the box if they are used to state *arguments*
for or against a topic (paragraphs 1 or 2 in the plan), or (o) if they are used to
express a writer's *opinion* (paragraph 3).

I believe that _____	First, _____	In my opinion _____
Moreover _____	The most important point is that _____	
It could be argued that _____		Third _____
I think _____	Also _____	Another point is that _____

B   Choose a suitable expression from the box for each gap in the following
answer to the essay title from 1 B.

In many countries parents are now choosing to educate their
children at home. This has a number of advantages. _____
parents may be able to provide a more practical education for
their children than schools can, and a more relaxing atmosphere
for study. _____ parents are in a better position to keep
their children away from bad influences if they can keep watch
over them at home. _____ parents know what is best for
their children.
However, there are many arguments in support of sending children
to school rather than educating them at home. Children are
isolated at home; at school they will become sociable, and
accustomed to meeting people independently. _____ schools
can provide trained teachers and good educational facilities.
_____ parents are too emotionally 'close' to their
children to make very good teachers.
_____ education at school is preferable to education at
home. There are special cases (for example, for disabled children)
in which home education is the only option; however, for the vast
majority of children greater benefits are gained by going to
school.

C   Choose one of the essay titles below. Write a 150-word essay, remembering to
plan and organise your answer, and use some of the expressions in the box.

All educational facilities should be funded by the government.

OR

To what extent is firm discipline a necessary part of teaching children?

▶ **R e a d i n g** *You are advised to spend about 20 minutes on questions 1-15.*

Part I

Questions 1-3

Answer these questions using Reading Passage 1.

1   Which ONE word from the text best describes the layer of gases around the earth?

   Your answer _____

2   What are the two main greenhouse gases mentioned?

   _____ and _____

3   'But one thing is clear – it will be no picnic' (paragraph 3). What is the purpose of this sentence? Choose the purpose from the four listed below, and write **A, B, C** or **D** in the space provided.

   A to identify a specific problem
   B to give a warning
   C to provide evidence for an earlier idea
   D to serve as an example

   Your answer
   _____

Reading Passage 1

The Greenhouse Effect

The greenhouse effect is not a new phenomenon. Scientists have known for centuries that a layer of gases naturally surrounds the earth like an insulating blanket, trapping the reflected energy of the sun and preventing it from escaping into space. That is what makes the earth warm enough for people, plants and animals. However, recent human activity has boosted concentrations of greenhouse gases and enhanced their heat-trapping ability. The main culprit is carbon dioxide (CO_2), which scientists estimate accounts for nearly half of global warming. CO_2 is released from burning fossil fuels (coal, oil and gas) and from clearing and burning forests.

There are other important greenhouse gases too and they cannot be ignored – CFCs for example may account for 25 per cent of global warming in the next century if their production is not scaled back. But carbon dioxide is the pivotal one. The UN International Panel on Climatic Change now says that CO_2 levels could double within 40 years if present rates of fossil-fuel burning and deforestation continue. That could mean an average temperature increase between two and four degrees centigrade and a sea-level rise of perhaps a foot by 2050.

No-one knows for certain how local weather will change as a result of this warming. But one thing is clear – it will be no picnic. Indications are that the earth will be warmer than at any time since the

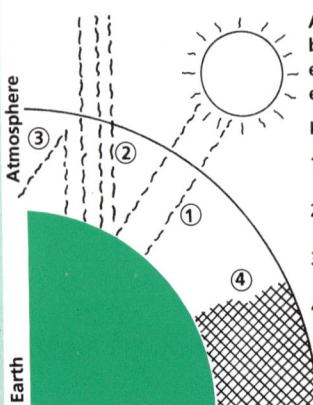

The Greenhouse Effect

A layer of gases in the atmosphere acts like an insulating blanket trapping solar energy that would otherwise escape into space. Without these 'greenhouse gases' the earth would be frozen, barren and lifeless.

HOW IT WORKS

1 Solar energy enters the atmosphere unaffected by greenhouse gases.
2 The sun's rays are absorbed by the earth, then reflected back at longer heat wavelengths.
3 Greenhouse gases absorb this heat, then send it back to the surface.
4 When greenhouse gas concentrations increase, more heat is captured causing temperatures in the lower atmosphere and surface to rise. This affects both weather and climate.

start of the last ice age nearly 10 0000 years ago. But there's one major difference. This temperature increase will take place not over thousands of years, but over decades. And it is the speed of the change which makes the precise impact so difficult to predict.

The most sophisticated computerized climate models, in the US and Britain, agree that weather around the world will become more erratic and more extreme. In general, temperatures will rise more towards the poles than at the equator. Overall rainfall will also increase as higher temperatures boost evaporation from the seas. But the distribution of precipitation will shift. Some areas will become wetter, others will be drier. In middle latitudes, climate zones will march pole-wards, Saskatchewan may become like Kansas, southern England

like southern France. In tropical and sub-tropical parts of the Third World warming will be less but the impact on a relatively stable climate will be greater. Tropical storms and droughts could both increase. The pattern of the monsoons may shift.

Global warming will also cause ocean levels to rise – though not, as popular wisdom has it, due to the Antarctic ice cap melting. If this catastrophe occurs it will not be for at least another century. Instead sea levels will rise simply because water expands as it warms. People living in low-lying coastal regions from New York and London to Jakarta and Dacca will be in danger. The world's great river deltas, home to millions in Asia and Latin America and containing some of the Third World's richest food-growing land, could become brackish graveyards.

Questions 4-15

The passage below is a SUMMARY of Reading Passage 1. Complete this summary by writing ONE or TWO words in each space. These words must be taken from the reading passage. The first one has been done as an example.

It has long been known that earth is __(Example)__ to support life because of an ____4____ layer of greenhouse gases which trap the sun's ____5____. Recently, increased production of one of these gases, ____6____ by mankind's ____7____ of wood and fossil fuels, has been the main cause of ____8____. If the ____9____ of CO_2 continue to increase both temperature and ____10____ could rise significantly by 2050. The ____11____ of this change has made predictions about the effect on the world's ____12____ uncertain. However, computers forecast greater unpredictability and a more ____13____ climate. And with the temperature rise will come a corresponding expansion of ____14____ and rising sea-levels, threatening ____15____ cities and fertile land alike.

Your answers

Example: <u>warm enough</u>   9 _____

4 _____   10 _____

5 _____   11 _____

6 _____   12 _____

7 _____   13 _____

8 _____   14 _____

15 _____

Part 2

Reading Passage 2   *You are advised to spend about 15 minutes on questions 16-25.*

Impact of global warming on climate

1 But there are also hidden factors which scientists call 'feedback mechanisms'. No-one knows quite how they will inter-act with the changing climate. Here's one example: plants and animals adapt to climate change over centuries. At the current estimate of half a degree centigrade of warming per decade, vegetation may not keep up. Climatologist James Hansen of the US space agency NASA predicts climate zones will shift toward the poles by 50 to 75 kilometres a year – faster than trees can naturally migrate. Species that find themselves in an unfamiliar environment will die. The 1000-kilometre-wide strip of coniferous forest running through Canada, the USSR and Scandinavia could be cut by half, setting in motion a chain reaction. Millions of dying and diseased trees would soon lead to massive forest fires, releasing tons of CO_2 and further boosting global warming.

2 There are dozens of other possible 'feedback mechanisms'. Higher temperatures will fuel condensation and increase cloudiness, which may actually damp down global warming. Others, like the 'albedo' effect, will do the opposite. The 'albedo' effect is the amount of solar energy reflected by the earth's surface. As northern ice and snow melts and the darker sea and land pokes through, more heat will be absorbed, adding inexorably to the global temperature increase.

3 Scientists continue to tinker away with their computer models, but the bare-bones facts are clear. Even if we were to magically stop all greenhouse-gas emissions tomorrow the impact on global climate would continue for decades. Delay, any delay, will simply make the problem worse. The fact is that some of us are doing quite well the way things are. In the developed world prosperity has been built on 150 years of cheap fossil fuels. Oil fires cars and powers industry, coal generates electricity and indirectly runs TVs, dishwashers and VCRs. Gas heats water and warms homes and factories.

4 Material progress has been linked to energy consumption. Today 75 per cent of all the world's energy is consumed by a quarter of the world's population. The average rich-world resident adds about 3.2 tons of CO_2 yearly to the atmosphere, more than four times the level added by each Third World citizen. India, China and Brazil, which make up nearly half the world's population, accounted for barely 15 per cent of global warming during the 1980s, according to the US Environmental Protection Agency. The US, with just seven per cent of the global population, is responsible for 22 per cent.

Questions 16-19

Answer these questions using Reading Passage 2.

Choose which of the alternatives is the correct answer and put the appropriate letter in the space provided.

Example: Feedback mechanisms are: **Your answers**

        A statistics.
        B concealed causes.
        C known results.
        D scientific methods.   _____B_____

16 In paragraph 1 the writer is:

        A rejecting a scientific belief.
        B giving an example.
        C reaching a conclusion.
        D defending a theory.   _____

17 If greenhouse gas emissions were stopped immediately, the world's climate:

        A would soon regain its balance.
        B would continue to be affected but without serious consequences.
        C would continue to be affected for many years to come.
        D would be affected for another 10 years.   _____

18 According to the writer cheap fossil fuels have:

        A formed the basis of the developed world's success.
        B contributed to the developed world's success.
        C aided the developed world's building trade.
        D caused 150 years of global warming.   _____

19 A person from a developing country:

        A adds more than 3 tons of CO_2 yearly to the atmosphere.
        B adds about 12.8 tons of CO_2 yearly to the atmosphere.
        C adds 4 tons of CO_2 yearly to the atmosphere.
        D adds less than a ton of CO_2 yearly to the atmosphere.   _____

Questions 20-25

Refer to Reading Passage 2. Show whether, **according to the text,** the following statements are true or false by circling **A** for True or **B** for False. If the passage does not say, circle **C**.

Statement	True	False	Does not say
20 James Hanson predicts that the shift in climate zones will be accompanied by a successful migration of trees.	A	B	C
21 Some factors may slow global warming.	A	B	C
22 The 'albedo effect' is measured in units of temperature.	A	B	C
23 The basic facts of global warming are unknown.	A	B	C
24 The developed world has decided to reduce its energy consumption.	A	B	C
25 The statistics in the last two sentences were supplied by the US Environmental Protection Agency.	A	B	C

Part 3

Reading Passage 3

Turning Up the Heat in the Greenhouse

For a country that produces more than 20 percent of the planet's greenhouse gases, the United States **(Example)** . But in a report a National Academy of Sciences panel warned that using the atmosphere as an industrial sewer could send temperatures soaring 2 to 9 degrees Fahrenheit in the near future – and called for measures that would __26__ . Says Yale University economist and panel member William Nordhaus, 'It is worth making modest investments today to slow climate change and prepare for it.'

How? The panel recommended phasing out chloro-fluorocarbons, __27__ .

Next comes energy efficiency. Replacing standard light bulbs with compact fluorescents that are more efficient and raising miles-per-gallon standards for new cars would more than pay for themselves – and cut the use of fuels that emit greenhouse gases. It urged lawmakers to raise energy prices, impose more efficient building codes, increase support for mass transit and __28__ . And it called on Americans to prepare for the side effects of a changing climate, for example by reducing the amount of wasted water, __29__ .

While they applauded the report, the environmentalists worried that its recommendations would meet with stiff resistance from the White House. Moreover, many scientists continue to doubt that global temperatures are rising at alarming rates – __30__ . Panel Member Jessica Tuchman Mathews, vice president of the World Resources Institute, concedes that the science of measuring climate changes __31__ . 'But when there's the potential for irreversible consequences,' she says, 'we have to act.' The question is whether the findings will be acted on, or just add to the hot air.

You are advised to spend about 15 minutes on questions 26-31.

Questions 26-31

Look at Reading Passage 3. Seven phrases have been left out. Decide which phrase from the list **A-I** below should go in each gap and write the letter in the space provided. Note that there are more phrases than gaps.

The first one has been done as an example.

Your answers

A boost efficiency standards for electrical appliances.

Example: ___E___

B reduce temperatures by a similar amount.

26 _____

C the chemicals that both destroy the ozone layer and heat the atmosphere.

27 _____

28 _____

D or even that the earth is warming at all.

29 _____

E has been slow to do much about global warming.

30 _____

F a major cause of the rise in sea-level.

31 _____

G is imprecise.

H cut greenhouse emissions 10 to 40 percent with minimal cost to the economy.

I which could become scarcer in the years ahead.

Writing   *You should spend no more than 30 minutes on this task.*

TASK   **Write an essay for a university teacher on the following topic:**

To what extent is the continuing use of fossil fuels and CFCs acceptable given the evidence of global warming?

In writing your essay, make sure that:

1   the essay is well organised,
2   your point of view is clearly expressed, and
3   your argument is supported by relevant evidence from the reading passages.

NOTE: Do not copy word-for-word from the reading passages.
   You should write at least 150 words.

▶ # Listening

Section 1

Questions 1-8

Listen to the two people discussing what's on, and fill in the gaps numbered 1-8 in the chart below.

What	Title	Where	Day	Time
The film	1	The Odeon	2	3
The play	4	5	Every day except 6	2.30 / 7.30
The talk	The good, the bad and the ozone	7	Wednesday	8

Section 2

Questions 9-18

Answer questions 9-18 by writing a word or short phrase in the space provided. The first one is done for you as an example.

Your answers

Example: Where is ozone found?   <u>the Earth's stratosphere</u>

 9 What does ozone filter out?   _____

10 Where is there a high level of concentration of ozone?   _____

11 What was London known as in the past?   _____

12 What was the major cause of London's smogs?   _____

13 What does sunlight encourage to turn into ozone?   _____

14 Give *two* examples of crops affected by too much ultra-violet radiation.   _____

15 What are malignant melanomas?   _____

16 Give *one* of the two vital properties of CFCs.   _____

17 About how long does it take CFCs to
    break down?   _____

18 When does chlorine become an
    ozone destroyer?   _____

Section 3

Questions 19-25

Fill in the gaps in the summary of the second part of the talk by writing in the
missing words in the columns to the right of the passage.

Your answers

Joe Farman first reported, in ___19___, a hole the size of the
US and as deep as Mount Everest (nearly ___20___ metres)
over Antarctica. Every November it breaks up into areas of
ozone-reduced air that ___21___ around the southern
hemisphere. These could cause a rise in cases of malignant
melanomas in humans and spread over a large ___22___ of
the earth. Few countries have taken steps to ___23___ CFCs.
Butane and propane have been suggested as replacements for
CFCs in ___24___, but carry a risk of ___25___. Some
scientists even claim that CFCs do less damage than other
gases produced by burning.

19 _____
20 _____
21 _____
22 _____
23 _____
24 _____
25 _____

 # Speaking

How optimistic – or pessimistic – do *you* feel about the future? Discuss these statements and questions with a partner; spend at least *two* minutes on each one.

- Humans have realised too late the environmental consequences of their activities.
- If scientists' predictions about global warming are accurate, how do you think your country will be affected?
- In the next 50 years, the world's population will start to decrease.
- Are there any ways that you personally can contribute to improving the environment?
- 'My children will inherit the consequences of our abuse of the world's resources.'

▶ # Key and feedback

Reading

Part 1 The Greenhouse Effect

1 blanket
2 CO_2 and CFCs
3 B

4 insulating
5 (reflected) energy
6 CO_2
7 burning
8 global warming
9 levels
10 sea-level
11 speed
12 weather
13 extreme
14 water
15 low-lying

In question 1 the word is not 'insulating': the word 'blanket' suggests insulation.

In question 3 the picnic sentence refers to the weather; we've already heard it's going to be uncertain, now we get a warning that it could be unpleasant.

If you found the summary difficult, look back at SKILLS FOCUS in Unit 6 - *Gap-filling Tasks*, page 74.

Part 2 Impact of global warming on climate

16 B
17 C
18 A
19 D

20 B
21 A
22 C
23 B
24 C
25 A

In question 16 the writer is giving an example. Can you identify the example? What is it an example of?

Questions 17,18,19 tested your recognition and understanding of key vocabulary; 17-'decades', 18-'built...on', and 19-'four times the level' ($3.2 \div 4 = 0.8$, which is less than a ton).

In questions 20-25 did you remember to follow this method?

Part 3 Turning Up the Heat in the Greenhouse

26 H
27 C
28 A
29 I
30 D
31 G

Scan or skim to find relevant passage

⬇

Read carefully every word of/around that passage.

Can't find any evidence: choose C

Read the statement again and answer A or B

For questions 26-31 a good method is to read around the gap and try to *predict* the missing information, *then* choose one from the options. Don't forget a grammar check: for example question 26 'would', a modal verb, is followed by an infinitive, limiting your choice to A, B, and H.

Writing

Self assessment: Did you do the usual checks?

Spend some time now assessing your essay. Do you think *now* that you approached your answer in the best way? If not, how should you have done it? What were the main points of:

- your introduction
- your main body
- your conclusion

Did you use information from the reading texts? Check you didn't copy word-for-word.

Listening

Section 1
1 Time off
2 Tuesday
3 9.30
4 Chicken
5 The Palace
6 Monday
7 The Town hall
8 7.00

Section 2
9 Ultraviolet radiation
10 Polluted cities
11 The Smoke
12 Coal-burning fires
13 oxygen
14 Any two of: maize, wheat, and rice
15 skin cancer(s)
16 One of: they do not burn
            they are not poisonous

17 75 years
18 In spring

For questions **9-18** notice that the correct answers are *short* answers; the question did not demand full sentences.

Section 3
18 1985
20 8850
21 drift
22 area
23 ban
24 refrigerators
25 fire

'refrigerator' is wrong for question **24** because of the structure of the sentence.

Speaking

Did you have enough ideas to spend two minutes on each statement or question? If it was difficult, why? Were the topics unfamiliar? Remember, you may be asked to talk about topics that are not directly related to your life or work in the IELTS interview.

You also had to *speculate* about the future: that is, make guesses and predictions, for example, about your country's future.
Did you follow-up your responses with suggestions about possible actions?
See SKILLS FOCUS in this unit - *Speaking: Speculating about the future*, page 122.

Skills Focus
Speaking - Speculating about the future

In the speaking section you had to *speculate* about the future, that is, make guesses and predictions.

A   Listen to someone discussing the final statement from the 'Speaking' section of this unit, page 118, and answer these two questions.

1   Do you think the man is optimistic or pessimistic about the future?
2   Did he make any points that you made when you talked about the same statement?

B   Now listen again, and complete these sentences he uses.

_____, I think it's _____ true.

I mean there _____ be any oil.

_____ our children _____ still have it.

I mean, I _____ it's true to say our children ...

But perhaps _____ that knowledge _____ enable to do something about it in future generations.

Study the language used in the above sentences.

Notice: • that we usually use 'will' to make predictions
          • that expressions such as 'well ... ' and 'I mean ... ' give you time to think
          • that 'I suppose', 'perhaps', and 'probably' are useful ways of expressing opinion without being too forceful. Of course, you can use 'I think' too!
          • the expression 'at least' in the final sentence. What is its purpose? Is it:

          A to say that the information following is unimportant
          B to say that this is the speaker's final point?
          C to say that there is *something* positive in a generally negative response?

C   See if you can use any of this language to talk about the following:

• How do you think the lives of your grandchildren will differ from your own?
• How will a better knowledge of English help you (or someone you know) in your present situation?

▶ **R e a d i n g**

You have 55 minutes to complete questions 1-39. Write your answers on the answer sheet which you will find at the end of the reading section.

You are advised to spend about 15 minutes on questions 1-13 which are based on Reading Passage 1.

Questions 1-4

Reading Passage 1, **Stay Awake, Stay Alive**, is divided into four sections. From the list of headings (**A-G**) below, choose the best heading for each section and write the corresponding letter in boxes 1 to 4 on your answer sheet. There are more headings than you need.

1 Section 1
2 Section 2
3 Section 3
4 Section 4

List of headings

A Unreliable data

B Sleeping while driving

C Government investigations

D Motorway accidents

E Identifying sleep-related accidents

F The reluctance of drivers to talk

G Lack of government support

Reading Passage 1

Stay Awake, Stay Alive

Section 1

Sleep laboratories around the world are finding that an alarming number of drivers on motorways may be falling asleep at the wheel. Although researchers have difficulty in knowing for certain whether an accident has been caused by sleepiness, it appears that a driver who is on the road between 4 am and 6 am is about 10 times as likely to have a sleep-related accident as someone who is driving in the middle of the morning or early in the evening. Some British police forces have become sufficiently concerned to launch campaigns to alert the public to the danger. Leicestershire police, for example, consider sleepiness to be the cause of 20 per cent of accidents on motorways and in the summer of 1990 ran a campaign with the slogan 'Stay Awake, Stay Alive'. Major motor manufacturers such as Ford and Renault are investigating ways of incorporating sleepiness detectors and alarms into their vehicles.

Section 2

However, British government bodies responsible for road safety have not initiated any studies into the problem of sleepy drivers on motorways. The Department of Transport claims that it is 'aware of the problems', but does not regard it as a high-priority issue and is not planning to support any relevant research apart from a general study on 'driver behaviour'. The department has no figures on the number of accidents caused by driver sleepiness and says it doubts whether reliable statistics can ever be obtained.

Section 3

Unfortunately, the issue is clouded by the fact that many motorway accidents that might be caused by sleepiness are categorised under other headings, such as 'inattention', 'failed to look or see other vehicle' and 'misjudged speed/distance'. Figures collected in the 1970s by the Transport and Road Research Laboratory list the cause of 20 per cent of all road accidents as 'perceptual errors'. 'Fatigue' was specified in only 2 per cent of cases. However, few investigators inquire further to discover just *why* a driver was not attending, failed to look or made errors in perception. For various reasons, including the fear of prosecution and possible difficulties with insurance claims, drivers are reluctant to admit to falling asleep, but are more willing to admit to 'inattention'. When these rather vague responses are examined thoroughly, sleepiness often emerges as the true culprit.

Section 4

Driving on a road as dull as a motorway exacerbates sleepiness in a driver who is already sleepy. But how can we tell if an accident on a motorway has been caused by sleepiness? There are some very strong pointers. If an accident involves only one vehicle, which runs off the road into the central crash barrier, the embankment, a tree or a bridge, then sleepiness is likely to be the cause, especially if there are no skid marks or other signs of braking. A driver who is alert to an impending crash grips the steering wheel and suffers different injuries from someone who is asleep and holding the steering wheel loosely. This pattern of injury, combined with an absence of skid marks on the road, also suggests that the driver was asleep in accidents where one vehicle runs into the back of another, especially if it occurs where traffic is light and vehicles are consequently well-spaced on the road. Under these conditions, the driver's 'inattention' must have been more than just momentary.

The passage on the next page is a summary of Reading Passage 1. Complete the summary by choosing ONE or TWO words *from the text* to fill in each gap. Write the answers on your answer sheet.

Summary of Reading Passage 1

Recent research shows that a __(Example)__ driving early in the morning ...

Answer: driver

Recent research shows that a __(Example)__ driving early in the morning is more ____5____ be involved in an accident caused by ____6____ than a driver driving during the middle of the morning or early evening. Police forces and ____7____ are trying to find ways to reduce the numbers of sleep-related accidents. However, the government does not seem to be sufficiently worried to invest in ____8____ and ____9____ the reliability of statistics. The statistics are difficult to gather because motorway accidents are often ____10____ under imprecise headings such as 'inattention', and investigators fail to ____11____ into the reason for inattention – which may be sleepiness. Various ____12____ at the scene of an accident, for example lack of evidence of ____13____ or certain injury patterns, reveal that sleep may have been the cause.

You are advised to spend about 20 minutes on questions 14-28 which refer to Reading Passage 2.

Questions 14-21

Complete the diagram below by selecting a maximum of four words *from the text* for each answer. Write the answers in boxes **14-21** on your answer sheet.

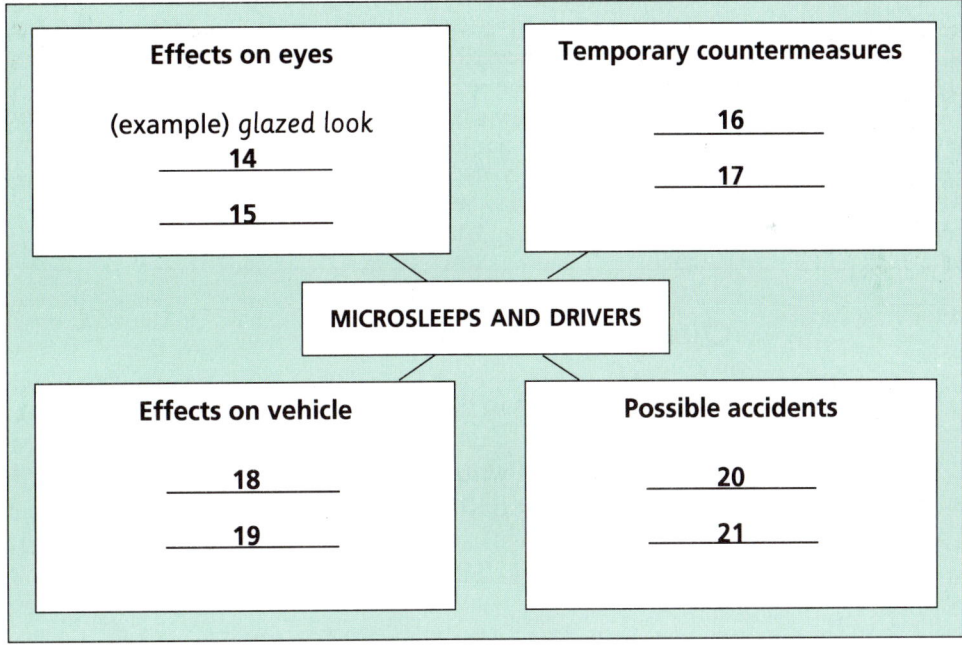

Effects on eyes

(example) glazed look
____14____
____15____

Temporary countermeasures

____16____
____17____

MICROSLEEPS AND DRIVERS

Effects on vehicle

____18____
____19____

Possible accidents

____20____
____21____

Reading Passage 2

Falling Asleep

What happens when you are falling asleep? As sleepiness increases, a glazed look comes over the eyes, visual awareness declines and 'eye-rolling' begins. The eyes roll up under the slowly closing eyelids, which then slowly open and the eyes roll back down again. One complete eye-roll lasts about two seconds, and is usually followed immediately by another. Such events are called 'microsleeps' where consciousness is clouding and the brain is losing contact with reality. It is possible to snap out of this state for a while. Drivers can open the car windows, turn up the radio and sing a song in the hope that all this stimulation will overcome the sleepiness. But for anyone who is really sleepy, such countermeasures are seldom effective for more than a few minutes. Microsleeps and eye-rolling reappear, maybe lasting for many seconds, interspersed with short bursts of greater alertness. Successive microsleeps get longer until true sleep sets in and the head lolls forward, causing, with luck, a startled awakening.

A driver having microsleeps is still vaguely aware of the road but is likely to misperceive events ahead. Limited driving skills can be maintained to keep the vehicle on a fairly straight course or carry out simple steering manoeuvres. Nevertheless, the vehicle may begin to drift sideways and foot-pressure on the accelerator may relax, causing the vehicle to slow down. The driver may still seem to be in control, but as microsleeps particularly impair vision, the immediate danger is one of collision or running off the road. Sleepy drivers tend to drive more slowly, anyway, and try to keep in the slow lane. When the vehicle drifts sideways the main risk is collision with a stationary vehicle on the hard shoulder.

It is known that the brain's 24-hour clock is set to bring sleep twice a day: at night, and in the early afternoon. The early afternoon is therefore a time that can produce a marked feeling of sleepiness, and this is not due to eating lunch. This is the period when sleep-related accidents reach their daytime peak. Many cultures, especially in hot countries, have bowed to the inevitable and adopted the siesta as a way of life. The time of greatest alertness, on the other hand, is in the early evening. Alcohol interacts with this daily rhythm to worsen afternoon sleepiness, which is why many people find that even two units of alcohol (equivalent to a pint of beer) at lunchtime have a strongly soporific effect. While this alcohol intake is unlikely to push drivers over the legal limit, a study showed that at this time of day it clearly impaired simulated motorway driving. The same alcohol intake in the early evening has the same effect on blood alcohol level but can go almost unnoticed, and driving will be less affected. This suggests there is a strong case for setting a lower legal blood alcohol limit for the early afternoon compared with that for the early evening. The more sleepy drivers are feeling, the more alcohol affects them. Tranquillisers can also be soporific, especially at the vulnerable times of the day. Little is known about whether they present a problem for monotonous driving, although many sleep researchers believe they do.

Questions 22 and 23

Write your answers in boxes 22 and 23 of your answer sheet.

22   What does the writer imply early afternoon sleepiness is often attributed to?
23   When do most daytime sleep-related accidents occur?

Questions 24-28

Complete the flow chart below with words from Reading Passage 2. You should use ONE or TWO words for each answer. Write them on your answer sheet.

Alcohol intake works together with ___(Example) daily rhythm___ .

↓

Increased sleepiness if drinking at _____24_____ .

↓

Deterioration in _____25_____ ability.

↓

Comparison with evening: alcohol has _____26_____ effect on blood,

_____27_____ effect on driving.

↓

Argument for change in legal limit of _____28_____ .

You are advised to spend about 20 minutes on questions 29-39 which are based on Reading Passage 3.

Reading Passage 3

Planes that Fall to Pieces

On April 28, 1988, the roof came off a Boeing 737 of Aloha Airlines while it was flying over Hawaii. In the explosive decompression that followed, a flight attendant was sucked out to her death and seven passengers were seriously injured, but miraculously the aircraft managed to land, 18 minutes later, without disintegrating.

It was a dramatic introduction to the phenomenon of the geriatric jet. Until then, few air travellers worried about the age of aircraft. It was generally assumed that international regulatory authorities insisted on rigorous maintenance and inspection procedures specifically designed to detect and prevent structural fatigue and corrosion.

Aloha Airlines aircraft number N73711 changed all that. It was discovered that rivets holding two sections of the fuselage together had blown and the bonding had failed. The cause: corrosion and metal fatigue. The plane was 19 years old and had completed 89 680 take-off and landing cycles. Its design life was 75 000 cycles. Nor was its age in any way unusual. Boeing produced figures this year showing that 558 of its aircraft were still in service beyond their 'economic design life objective' of 20 years.

Ensuring aircraft are safe to fly depends on a crucial troika: the national regulatory authority, which grants airworthiness certificates; the aircraft manufacturer, which issues technical instructions for the maintenance, inspection and replacement of parts; and the airline, which is supposed to carry out the manufacturers' instructions.

In the case of N73711, Aloha Airlines' maintenance procedures were seriously deficient. Its aircraft were overworked on short, island-hopping flights and were exposed to a corrosive salt atmosphere, yet its corrosion control programme was inadequate. Boeing, which had discovered the problems at Aloha, had failed to alert the FAA.

With a worldwide shortage of new aircraft and an ever-ageing fleet, it was realised belatedly that growing numbers of elderly aircraft were going to pose problems hitherto unforeseen – like the need to check 70 000 rivets, rivet by rivet, on other geriatric jets.

'We no longer believe you can rely on inspections forever as aircraft approach their life-limit goal,' says Tom Swift, a British-born metallurgist at the FAA. 'We think it is important to establish a point at which you must start replacing parts.'

A particular recent concern is the phenomenon of 'multi-site damage', when hairline cracks develop behind a row of rivets and create a fault that can rip apart like serrated paper. MSD was identified as the cause of the crash of the Japanese Airlines Boeing 747 in 1985, when 520 people lost their lives.

In Britain, the CAA has a good record for upholding high standards of aircraft maintenance, insisting on fatigue testing of every fuselage and pioneering the concept of structural audits to find fault at an early stage. Nevertheless, Ronald Ashford, the director of safety, admits that there were shortcomings. 'In future there will be much more rigorous inspection programmes and a greater tendency to require replacement of large areas of frames and skins.'

Questions 29-33

Decide whether the statements are, according to the text, true, false or the information is not given and write **A** for true, **B** for false, and **C** for not given, on your answer sheet.

29 In the Aloha Airlines accident the roof blew off because of explosive decompression in the plane.
30 According to the writer it is remarkable that the aeroplane did not break apart before landing.
31 The cause of the Aloha Airlines accident was never discovered.
32 Many old aircraft still in use beyond their 20-year-limit have passed Boeing fitness tests.
33 The safety of aircraft depends on, among other things, the airline following the instructions given by the aircraft manufacturer.

Questions 34-39

34 and 35 What TWO factors made Aloha Airlines aircraft deteriorate especially quickly?
Write the answers in boxes **34** and **35** of your answer sheet.

36 Tom Swift says that as planes approach their 'life-limit goal':

A they should be replaced.
B they should increase the numbers of inspections.
C a decision should be made about when to replace, instead of fix, whole parts.
D certain parts should be replaced.

Write the appropriate letter (**A, B, C** or **D**) in box **36** on your answer sheet.

37 According to the information in the text, multi-site damage:

A has only recently been discovered.
B is of particular concern now.
C has been the cause of several airline accidents.
D can rip apart like serrated paper.

Write the appropriate letter (**A, B, C** or **D**) in box **37** on your answer sheet.

38 and 39 What TWO maintenance procedures are carried out by the CAA in Britain? Use two words from the text for each answer and write them in boxes **38** and **39** on your answer sheet.

Reading answer sheet

Write your answers to the reading section of this unit in the table below.

1		21	
2		22	
3		23	
4		24	
5		25	
6		26	
7		27	
8		28	
9		29	
10		30	
11		31	
12		32	
13		33	
14		34	
15		35	
16		36	
17		37	
18		38	
19		39	
20			

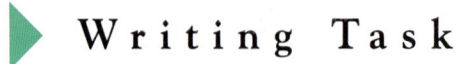

Writing Task 1

You should spend no more than 15 minutes on this task.

The table shows factors which affect the likelihood of a sleep-related road accident.

TASK **Describe the factors affecting the likelihood of a sleep-related road accident using the information in the table.**

Factors		Number of sleep-related accidents (Total 1000)
Roads:	Town	63
	Country	607
	Motorway	330
Time of day:	0 - 2.00	138
	4 - 6.00	280
	10 - 12.00	25
	14 - 16.00	153
	20 - 22.00	19
Age of driver:	Below 45	390
	Above 45	610

Writing Task 2

You should spend no more than 30 minutes on this task.

Reading Passage 1 describes how sleepiness may be responsible for many road accidents.

 **TASK** **Write an essay for a university teacher on the following topic:**

How far is it the responsibility of governments to reduce the number of road accidents which occur per year?

You should write at least 150 words.

You may use ideas from the reading passages but do NOT copy word-for-word. You should also use your own knowledge and ideas.

Listening

Section 1   Questions 1-6

Listen to Janet and Paul talking about a competition, and choose the best alternative, **A, B, C** or **D**, and circle the letter. The first one has been done for you as an example.

Example: How did Janet know about tonight's competition?

    A from television
    (B) from a poster
    C from a friend
    D from Paul

1 How were the members of Paul's team chosen?

    A they are friends
    B they are studying the same subject
    C according to competition rules
    D according to their interests

2 How long has the competition been going on?

    A four weeks
    B two weeks
    C since the previous term
    D since the start of term

3 What was unusual about the third round of the competition?

    A Paul's team won
    B Paul's team was disqualified
    C the other team was disqualified
    D the other team won

4 Where is the competition taking place tonight?

    A on the ground floor
    B Laboratory 2 of the medical building
    C the old lecture room of the medical building
    D the main lecture room of the medical building

5 What time will it probably start?

    A 8 pm
    B just after 8 pm
    C just before 8 pm
    D 9.30 pm

6 What does Paul say about tickets?

    A Janet should buy them at the university shop.
    B Janet should go to the competition without tickets.
    C Janet does not need tickets.
    D The competition is sold out.

Section 2 Questions 7-16

A policeman comes to Janet's college to give security advice. As you listen, fill in each gap **7-16** in Janet's notes with ONE or TWO words.

Bicycles *Bring your bike to a police station where they will* <u>7   </u> *a serial number on it and* <u>8   </u> *it on the police list. Get a good lock, or two locks, one for each* <u>9   </u>*; cheap locks are easy to cut. Lock the bike to something* <u>10   </u>*, report thefts immediately.*

Housing *College: doors have two locks so always* <u>11   </u> *your door, even when going out briefly. Close windows, and use window locks if you have them. Insure and register* <u>12   </u> *equipment. Private: get a good lock, check how many people have a* <u>13   </u>*. Keep windows closed. Get a* <u>14   </u> *for the door.*

Personal *Avoid walking* <u>15   </u> *late at night, and avoid dark streets. Carry a whistle. For a late night take* <u>16   </u> *money for a taxi or stay at a friend's house. Take self defence classes. Sensible precautions can prevent serious problems!*

Section 3 Questions 17-25

Listen to a student explaining to Janet how to use a computer, and decide if statements **17-25** are TRUE, FALSE or if the information is NOT GIVEN on the tape. Write T, F or NG in the box provided.

17 You need to switch the computer on in two places. ☐

18 The 'menu' tells you how to use the computer. ☐

19 Janet has been told she must type all her essays. ☐

20 You can start typing when you see an empty screen. ☐

21 An arrow on the screen shows you where mistakes are. ☐

22 Above the keyboard there are some words providing guidance. ☐

23 Most people use their name to name documents. ☐

24 Pressing 'y' means 'yes'. ☐

25 The student tells Janet how to exit from the computer. ☐

Section 4 Questions 26-33

Paul is talking to Janet about a year she spent travelling. As you listen, answer questions **26-33** by writing a word or short phrase in the space provided.

26 What was Janet's job in New Zealand? _____

27 Why did she work in New Zealand? _____

28 How did she travel within Indonesia? _____

29 How does Janet sum up Singapore? _____

30 How did she feel about the length of
time she had in China? _____

31 Why was she lucky to get into Tibet? _____

32 How long did she trek in Nepal? _____

33 What was her attitude to travel by the
end of her trip? _____

Key and feedback

Reading

1 Stay Awake, Stay Alive

1 B

2 G

Not C - the government has *failed* to investigate.

3 A

4 E

5 likely to

Did you include 'to'? It is essential for the sentence to make sense.

6 sleep(iness)

7 motor manufacturers

8 research

9 doubts

10 categorised

11 inquire (further)

12 pointers

What do you think 'pointers' means here? Use the context to guess.

13 braking

2 Falling Asleep

in either order:

14 visual awareness declines;

15 eye-rolling begins

any two, in any order, from:

16 open the windows;

17 turn up the radio;

sing a song

in either order:

18 drift sideways;

19 slow down

in either order:

20 collision;

21 running off the road

22 lunch

Notice the writer only *implies* this: '...and this is not due to eating lunch'

23 the early afternoon

24 lunchtime

25 (motorway) driving

26 (the) same

27 less

28 blood alcohol

3   **Planes that Fall to Pieces**

29 B

30 A

31 B

32 C

33 A

Check that you used A, B or C to answer these, and not T, F and NG.

in either order:

34 overworked aircraft/short flights;

35 corrosive salt atmosphere

36 C

37 B

in either order:

38 fatigue testing;

39 structural audits

Writing

It would be useful if a teacher could look at your answers to the writing tasks in this unit, and provide comments.

Task 1

From the table we can see that the most sleep-related accidents (i) occur on country roads, (ii) happen early in the morning, and (iii) involve older drivers. Did your answer reach the same conclusions? You needed to find expressions to refer to the *figures* in the table – here are some possible ones you might have included:

> 607 **per** thousand happen on country roads.
> Only 25 **out of** 1000 sleep-related accidents occur from 10-12 am.
> **About a third** of the accidents are on motorways.
> Older drivers have **more** accidents **than** young ones: 610 per thousand accidents compared to 390.

Task 2

Make sure you answered the question. The question was *not* asking you to say how the number of accidents can be reduced, but was about whose *responsibility* it is to reduce this number. Here are some points we thought of; compare them against your own.

Why it is the responsibility of governments

- they have the resources
- they own/build the roads
- they are able to train, educate people about road safety
- they can make and enforce road/vehicle laws
- governments represent people

Why it is the responsibility of individuals/others

- everybody needs to be aware of road dangers
- safe driving is an individual responsibility
- individuals/groups can influence a government

Listening

Section 1

1 A
2 D
3 C
4 C
5 B
6 B

Section 2

7 stamp
8 register
9 wheel
10 permanent
11 double lock
12 expensive
13 key
14 safety chain
15 alone
16 enough

Section 3

17 T
18 F
19 NG
20 T
21 F
22 T
23 NG
24 T
25 F

Section 4

26 secretary (in insurance company)
27 to raise money for travel
28 flying and boats
29 a great big shopping centre
30 too short / not enough time
31 it was closed to tourists
32 a week
33 (she was) ready to stop

Speaking

If you have a teacher and were interviewed, your teacher will have given you comments on your interview performance.

Reading and Listening: Score Guide

As this unit is not a real IELTS test, and as you may not have done it under test conditions, we cannot give you an exact IELTS 'band' corresponding to your score. However, the following guide to the reading and listening tests may give you a rough idea of your ability.

Reading

If you scored:

15 or fewer   you have made a good attempt at a difficult paper, but would benefit from further reading practice in English before taking your IELTS test.

16 to 27   you have reached a fair level of ability in reading English, and should do well in the reading part of your IELTS test. You would still benefit from more practice, however.

28 or more   reading English is a strong point of yours, and you might wish to concentrate on improving your other skills.

Listening

If you scored:

13 or fewer   you are still finding this part of the test difficult, and should try to listen to as much English as possible before taking the IELTS test.

14 to 24   you listen well in English, and are likely to achieve an adequate score in the IELTS listening test. However, you could improve further by continuing to listen to English as much as possible.

25 or more   you are a competent listener in English, and should do well in the IELTS listening test.

TAPESCRIPT

Unit 1   Listening

Bill Harvey has recently arrived in Britain to take up a place at Newcastle University. He has now arrived at the reception at his Hall of Residence. Stop the tape for one minute and look at the example and questions 1-4 in your book.

For each of the questions, four pictures are given. Decide which of the pictures best fits what you hear and circle **A, B, C,** or **D**. We have done the first one for you to show you what you have to do. Listen carefully.

Bill (B):	Hello.
Receptionist (R):	Oh, hello, you must be a new student. Did you find us OK?
B:	Well ... I got a bit lost and I had to ask a stranger, but I got here eventually.
R:	Oh dear. Have you come far today?
B:	Only from London – I was staying with my brother-in-law.
R:	Oh good. How did you get here?
B:	My brother-in-law took me to the railway station, and I got a bus at this end.
R:	Uh-huh. Well, you'd better tell me your name so I can find your form.
B:	It's Bill Harvey.
R:	Harvey ... Harvey ... ah yes. Oh, you've changed since this photo! What happened to your beard and moustache? And you're not wearing glasses either.
B:	No, I thought I'd better look smarter!
R:	Here's the key to your room – it's 422.
B:	Thanks. How do I get there?
R:	Go to the end of this corridor, turn right, and it's the second door on the left.
B:	Thank you. Oh ... there's a meeting for new students. I understand. What time is that?
R:	Half past four in the Common Room.
B:	Thanks a lot. Bye!

Unit 2   Listening

The director of an engineering company is interviewing an applicant for a job. Stop the tape for one minute and study the form on page 22.

Now listen to the interview and fill in the gaps numbered 1-10.

Director (D):	Ah, good morning. It's Mr Robinson, isn't it? Have a seat. *Steven* Robinson.
Applicant (A):	Yes.
D:	Is that S-T-E-V-E-N or P-H?
A:	It's 'V'.
D:	OK. I've got your letter of application, but I need a few more

	details for the file. Now, you're from Manchester – what exactly is the address?
A:	Yes, it's Dynevor Gardens. That's D-Y-N-E-V-O-R, Prestwich.
D:	Thanks. And telephone?
A:	Well, it isn't mine, it's the landlord's, but I can be contacted. It's 483 250.
D:	Uh-huh. The landlord lives in, does he?
A:	Well, he has the flat downstairs, and he's a friend of the family anyway.
D:	I see. OK. According to your letter I imagine you were born in, er, let me see, 1960?
A:	61.
D:	Right ... and the date?
A:	12th July.
D:	Thank you. And I believe you're married.
A:	No, no. I'm *getting* married, but not for a few months.
D:	Oh, sorry. Well, I mean congratulations! Is it going to be in Manchester?
A:	Well no actually. My fiancee's from Wales, so we're getting married in her home village, near Bangor.
D:	Oh, how nice ... now, as you know, when you apply for a post with Williams Engineering we need to find out a few things about both your academic background and more recent work experience, the latter being especially important in respect of this rather specialised position in the area of water management. First of all, A levels?
A:	Yes, I've got three. Geography, maths and physics.
D:	Geography, maths and physics. OK. And what about your degree?
A:	I went to Sheffield University and got an engineering degree, with water management as my specialisation.
D:	Uh-huh.
A:	And as for work experience ... I started out after graduating in 1986, in China, working for the Chinese Government.
D:	Did you work as a volunteer?
A:	No, I did get a nominal salary. It was a two-year irrigation project.
D:	That sounds fascinating. How did you organise that? You say it wasn't a British company then.
A:	No, no. My university had links with a Chinese engineering university, so it was organised at that level.
D:	And after that?
A:	Then I came back, moved to Manchester and have been working with Latimer Engineering since then.
D:	And what exactly are you doing for Latimer?
A:	Oh, I'm working in irrigation again, this time as a project research assistant.
D:	Great. I've got your details – now let's move on to a more general discussion about what we're looking for here ...

Unit 3   Listening

Clare and Jeremy have just spent an hour looking around a zoo. As you listen, decide if the statements are true, false, or the information is not mentioned and write T, F, or NM.

Now stop the tape for one minute and study the statements.
Listen and decide if the statements are true, false or not mentioned.

Clare (C): Well, it's pretty well laid out, I admit, and it's sort of attractive, but in the end I still find it a pretty depressing place.

Jeremy (J): Do you? Why?

C: Well, you know, animals out of their natural environment. They're just here for humans to look at. There's nothing natural about it.

J: Yeah, but if we didn't have any zoos a lot of species would just, well, they'd face extinction.

C: Do you really believe that?

J: Well, don't you? I mean they have good breeding projects for some species that are just dying out. Um, anyway, I think, you know, there's a trend towards developing zoos to become um ... education centres, you know, stimulating information for kids and displays, and that kind of thing.

C: Yeah, I know they've got lots of ideas, but these ideas are just because in the end zoos are outdated aren't they? And people are just trying to keep them going. And I don't think those projects you mentioned, those breeding projects, I don't think they're really successful. Animals just don't really want to breed in captivity. What we need to do is take care of the natural environment, make sure that they've still got a place where they can live in the wild.

J: Well, yeah, OK. But it's just not happening is it? Governments don't want to give the natural environment a chance. They want the wood in it, the forest, whatever, they want to grow crops. I mean it just doesn't happen. I think in reality you've got to have zoos.

C: Well, I just can't agree with that. I mean, I know all the points, but in the end humans just end up abusing animals for their own benefit. And zoos are just a pleasure park, aren't they? I mean, but, what is the pleasure in watching animals pacing up and down the cages?

J: Well look, I mean, zoos are changing. OK, some older zoos, it's animals in cages, but what about safari parks? You know, the animals are OK. They've got a lot of space, um, people see them in a much more natural setting. Um ... I think people learn about them and that means that they respect animals and it's probably in the end much better for animals that humans respect them in that way.

C: Well, maybe you're right, but I just can't agree with zoos.

Skills Focus   Listening for gist

Practice 1

As you listen to the following dialogues, write a short telegram with the main points. The first one is an example.

A: Oh Jack, I'm so excited. When do you think is a good time for it?
B: I don't know, what about July? The weather should be nice then.
A: OK, I'd better let my parents know. They'll be so pleased when they hear we're getting married.
B: Well, let's tell everybody now that we've decided.

1
A: I've got my ticket for London.
B: Great! When are you going then?
A: On the 14th September. I can't wait.
B: Is it to Heathrow or Gatwick airport?
A: Heathrow, and it gets in at 12.30 lunch time, so my mother should be able to meet me if I let her know.
B: Oh, lucky you.

2
A: Hey Andrew, we've just received that order of books from MacPherson and Co.
B: Great news. They finally got here. Did the deliverers have any explanation about the delay?
A: Yes, they said the ship got held up in Bombay. Anyway, they're here now so we can get going on the Team Report.
B: Yes. Oh, and we'd better inform MacPherson that they've arrived safely.

3
A: So what exactly happened then?
B: Well, I was in the market, you know, it's really crowded, and when I put my hand in my pocket I realised that my wallet had gone.
A: How much was in it?
B: Everything!
A: What are you going to do?
B: I'm going to have to ask my parents to wire me some money immediately.

Practice 2

As you listen to the three extracts decide who is speaking in each case.

1   First of all you should read pages 104 to 110, and take notes. Then I want you to write an essay of 150 words. I will collect them in on Thursday.

2   We do have quite a lot of problems at this time of year. I suppose because the weather's nice, people go out more, and leave their homes unattended, which is just what the burglars want.

3   Oh, yes, my son's doing really well now. He's a teacher you know, and loves his work. He teaches history and English.

Unit 4   Listening

As you listen to the following dialogue, fill in the spaces to complete the notes.

A: What are you reading, Frank?

B: It's this week's *New Scientist*, why?

A: I was just wondering – it looks interesting, but I've never actually read it myself. Is it aimed at real scientists or can ordinary people like me understand it?

B: Oh, it's for anyone really. It usually has articles and stories about current affairs as they relate to science, as well as papers about new breakthroughs in research. So some bits are easier for non-scientists to understand than others. I'm reading about a new telephone that allows you to see the person you're speaking to as well as hear them.

A: Oh I've heard about them. What does the article say then? Are they on the market yet? Can I buy one?

B: No, not this one. But the company, GPT, have made several prototypes to try out on businesses. This prototype is special because it's colour and the image is moving. You see, the first 'videophones' – that's what they're called – were made in Japan, but they can only show a still black and white image, so this videophone is much better than that. Mind you, I'm not sure I'd want one. Would you?

A: Well, no I don't think I would. I bet it costs a lot of money. Does it say how much it costs?

B: Yes, the early black and white ones cost several hundred pounds, but the one the story is about costs several thousand pounds!

A: Hmm, why does anybody want one, do you think?

B: From what I understand, the telephone company doesn't really know who will use them but they think the main customer is going to be business organisations that need constant link-ups with overseas organisations, and with this machine, (assuming the other organisation has got a videophone too) it's more like meeting face-to-face than a conversation on the telephone normally is, so maybe a lot of overseas travel can be avoided.

A: Yes, I suppose it would help cut down on travelling. But I still think most companies would prefer *really* meeting face-to-face than this video image thing.

B: Well, we'll see. Do you want to read the magazine?

A: Yes, when you've finished it I'd be quite interested.

Speaking

As you listen to these two descriptions, decide which is clearer.

Speaker 1:
Well, first you sit a written test and when you've finished that … er … the teacher marks it. And then you go to another room – oh! I didn't say did I – when you do your written test, you go to one room which is marked in reception – there's a map, and you sit your written test there and you wait in that room as the teacher marks it. Then you go to another room for your oral test and you sit your oral, oh – you don't sit it right away, you probably have to wait for a while. And then you have your oral which is five minutes. When that's finished you move on to reception, and you pay your money if you want to. Oh! When you've had your oral the teacher gives you a mark and that gives you your level, so when you go to

reception they know what your level is and tell you what class you're going to be in.

Speaker 2:

Okay. As you can see you've got twelve pieces. Your opponent also has twelve pieces of a different colour. The object is to move all your pieces into the spaces in which your opponent's pieces are now. And your opponent will be trying to move his or her pieces into your spaces. The winner is the first person to locate all their pieces in their opponent's spaces. You move by moving one piece one space at a time or, much quicker, you can jump over your own pieces or your opponent's pieces.

Unit 5   Listening

Simon, Daniel and Gill are studying environmental chemistry at university. They have been asked to submit a report to their tutor regarding the recycling of plastics. Now they are discussing their own views about the subject in the student canteen.

Simon (S):	If you actually think about how much plastic we use everyday it's astounding. I mean, look at this table now – the cups are plastic disposable ones, the sugar shaker is made of plastic, the ash trays are plastic, the packets of salt and pepper are plastic – the list is endless. And the awful thing about it all is that we know that when your average household throws away their rubbish the plastics just sit there for centuries, undegradable.
Gill (G):	Well, you're right, Simon, that plastic is everywhere, but I don't think you're right when you say that the discarded plastic just sits there for centuries without biodegrading. I think the majority of today's plastics do, in fact, break down reasonably quickly.
Daniel (D):	What do you mean by reasonably quickly then?
G:	Well, I don't know exactly – I suppose a couple of years.
S:	Come on Gill, do you really think that a couple of years is 'reasonably quickly'? I think it's pretty shocking to think of that waste just sitting there not biodegrading properly. What's needed is a new kind of plastic or something that breaks down at a much faster rate. Don't you think so Daniel?
D:	Actually I think you're both on the wrong track. What we need to be putting our energy into is recycling plastic, not throwing it away at all. Every time we throw away a plastic bottle or a plastic container, we are throwing away some of the world's valuable resources in the form of oil. We can't go on like this, we've got to start taking recycling seriously. Don't you agree with me?
S:	You're right, but are you realistic? Recycling, in an ideal world, is a great idea, but people just aren't going to do it are they? It's so much easier to just get rid of something in the dustbin than to take it to some special recycling depot. So we do need to make sure that we allow the waste products to be reabsorbed into the soil and atmosphere rather than just being a terrible sight for all.
G:	You know what the answer is then, don't you? We do both. We recycle the plastic that is easy to recycle, and make the rest easily biodegradable.
S:	What plastic products do you have in mind that are easy to recycle?

G: Shampoo bottles, detergent bottles, medicine bottles, food containers etc. They are all easily collectable and reusable.

D: You're right there, but actually I think you are missing the point of recycling. It doesn't just mean using old bottles again and again for the same purpose. What it means these days is melting the plastics down and building them up again into some completely new product such as a car or a park bench. That's where the future of recycling lies, not in the old 'use it again' idea.

S: Hey, look at the time, I've got to go. Seems a shame to break up the conversation, but I mustn't miss my lecture. What are you two doing now?

G: I'm going to the lab for a while.

D: And believe it or not I'm going to the library. Look, why don't we meet up for a drink later?

S: Yes, good idea. I'm meeting John anyway at the new bar in George Street. Have you been there yet?

D: No I haven't. What time will you be there?

S: At 8. What about you Gill?

G: I can't. I said I'd play squash tonight.

S: Oh, well, see you tomorrow then.

G: Yes, bye.

Skills Focus - Listening for specific information

Listen to the broadcast and answer the questions.

Good evening. This is the nine o'clock news. First the headlines. A gas explosion in Southern France is believed to have killed more than 40 people. The cause of the explosion is still being investigated. Three aid workers were killed when guerrillas attacked a convoy of trucks trying to deliver food to the besieged city of Barkov early this morning. All three of the workers were from France. Pakistan has won the third cricket test at Headingley after a thrilling tenth wicket partnership. And Prince Andrew has finally opened the new bridge over the Thames at Greenwich. Now those stories in more detail ...

Unit 6   Listening

Section 1

Mark and Jane are studying in Britain. They are at London's King's Cross station and want to go to Edinburgh. Stop the tape for one minute and look at the example and questions 1-4 in your book.

For each of the questions, four pictures are given. Decide which of the pictures best fits what you hear and circle **A, B, C** or **D**. We have done the first one for you to show you what you have to do. Listen carefully.

Mark (M): Oh, this station is enormous. Let's ask someone where the ticket office is?

Jane (J): OK. Er ... Excuse me, where can we buy tickets for Edinburgh?

Porter: Oh, you want the ticket office. It's just over there, do you see, between the snack bar and the newsagents?

J:	Oh yes. Thanks very much.
	Come on then.
M:	Oh look at the queues. It's so busy here. I wonder how long we'll have to wait. Which window shall we go for?
J:	Well there are five people in this one and seven in that one, so let's join the shorter one shall we!

Ticket clerk is TC.

J:	Nearly there. Oh. Hmm. Hello. Can we have two tickets to Edinburgh please?
TC:	Certainly. One way or are you coming back?
J:	Well, we'll be coming back on Wednesday.
TC:	OK, fine. That'll be £79 each.
J:	Oh, we've got student cards, does that reduce the price?
TC:	Oh yes. In that case it's, um, £52.65 each.
J:	Here you are.
TC:	And here are your tickets.
J:	Thanks. Oh, and one more thing. Could you tell us what time it goes?
TC:	Well, they go every hour, on the hour, so the next one's in 10 minutes at 12.00.
M:	Come on then, Jane, let's go. We'd better check the platform number on the board.
J:	There it is – Edinburgh, platform 6.
M:	No, that's arrivals. We go from 8. Shall we have a cup of coffee first?
J:	No, we haven't got much time. We'll get one on the train.

Section 2

Now look at Section 2.

When Mark and Jane arrived in Edinburgh, they discovered that Mark had left his camera on the train. At the Lost and Found office he has to fill in a Lost Property form. As you listen to the recording fill in the gaps numbered 5-10 on the form. First stop the tape for one minute and study the form.

Now listen carefully and fill in the gaps numbered 5-10.

Lost property officer is LPO.

LPO:	Good evening sir. Can I help you?
M:	Yes, I think I left my camera on the train from London earlier today.
LPO:	Did you sir? Oh well, in that case we'd better.fill in a Lost Property form. Can you tell me your name?
M:	Yes, it's Mark Adams.
LPO:	OK. Your address?
M:	You mean in Britain, or in the States?
LPO:	How long are you staying?
M:	Oh, I've still got a few months in Britain.
LPO:	OK then, can you give me your address here?
M:	Right. It's 21, Thames Drive, Leigh-on-Sea – that's L-E-I-G-H on Sea, Essex. Do you want the phone number?
LPO:	Yes, I'd better have that.
M:	OK, 0702 35211.

LPO:	Thanks. And you say it was a camera. What make and model?
M:	It's a Ricoh.
LPO:	Ricoh? How do you spell that?
M:	R-I-C-O-H.
LPO:	OK, got that. Now, you say it was the London train. What time did it arrive in Edinburgh?
M:	At 4.55 this afternoon, exactly on time.
LPO:	Well then, if we find it sir, shall we phone you?
M:	No, I think I'll drop in the day after tomorrow to check up.
LPO:	Right you are sir. We'll do our best.

Unit 7   Listening

Section I

Mrs Walker has just been admitted to hospital and a nurse is giving her information about rules and hospital life. Stop the tape for one minute and look at questions 1-8 in your book.

As you listen to the recording decide if the following statements are true or false and circle T for true and F for false. Listen carefully.

Nurse (N):	So Mrs Walker, this is your bed, and as you can see there are seven other beds in the ward. Have you got everything you need?
Mrs W:	Yes, I think so. I followed the hospital's advice and I've only brought a few belongings with me.
N:	Good – you can see the reasons why we ask you to do that, the cupboard is really very small. And have you arranged for anyone to bring in changes of nightwear and other clean clothes?
Mrs W:	Yes, my husband will deal with all that. Can you tell me what the visiting hours are?
N:	Yes, of course. They're in the afternoon from 2.30 to 3.30 and in the evening from 7 to 8, but remember that only two people can see you at the same time. Sorry about that but you can imagine the chaos if we didn't have these rules!
Mrs W:	Yes, I suppose so. What other rules are there?
N:	Well, first of all I should tell you about our hours. We start pretty early – you might not be used to that. We wake you at 6 o'clock, and breakfast is at 8 o'clock, lunch is at noon, there's tea at 3.30 and supper is at 6 o'clock.
Mrs W:	Oh my goodness! That's very different from what I've been used to. Still, I won't be here for long I hope. You'd better tell me the rest of the rules.
N:	Yes, well you can see the no smoking sign – we don't allow smoking on the wards under any circumstances, and the same goes for alcohol. I'm sure you understand why. However, if you do need to smoke there are special lounges where it's allowed.
Mrs W:	Oh, I don't smoke, so it doesn't affect me, and I think it's a jolly good rule. Do you smoke nurse?
N:	Er, no, but I used to – I've just given up in fact. I haven't had a cigarette for three months now.
Mrs W:	Well done! Look, I mustn't keep you any longer, but just one more question – can I make a telephone call, I mean, is there a phone

anywhere?

N: Yes, of course there is. Outside the ward there's a payphone. You need change for that of course. Oh, and that reminds me ... can you make sure that only *one* of your relatives or friends phones in each day to find out how you are? The switchboard gets clogged up with callers.

Mrs W: Yes, OK.

N: I must go and see how the other patients are doing now. You get changed and into bed, and I'll check on you in a while. The radio controls are here, with your own headphones, if you want to listen. It's our own hospital radio.

Mr W: Thanks very much. You've been very helpful.

That is the end of Section 1. Stop the tape and check your answers for half a minute.

Section 2

Now look at Section 2.

Mrs Walker is listening to the hospital radio. As you listen to the recording fill in the gaps numbered 9-16 by writing in the missing words in the column to the right of the passage. Stop the tape for one minute and study questions 9-16.

Now listen carefully and answer questions 9-16

Introducer: Welcome to radio Henton – the radio station specially for you. It's four o'clock and time for our look at Henton Hospital and its history. And here to tell you about it is Janet Newman. Hello Janet.

Janet: Hello Mike, and hello listeners. Yes, I'm going to tell you a little bit about our hospital – to you maybe it's just four white walls and a ceiling, but this hospital has a history going back three quarters of a century. It was built in 1924 and was designed to sleep 200 patients. The original building is now the Jones Building, named after the architect Thomas Jones, so those of you listening in wards A to H are in the oldest part of the building. The physiotherapy department is also there. They started building the new block in 1958, so that now the hospital can sleep 800 patients. It started its life as an ordinary general hospital, but after the completion of the new part, in 1963 – yes it took five years – it became the teaching hospital that it is famous for today. Every year a hundred new medics are registered with us – you've probably seen some of them coming round – and we have one of the highest success rates amongst teaching hospitals. We also have a school of nursing and physiotherapy. They're in the low building behind the radiography department. Henton Hospital has also recently become famous for its successes in open heart surgery, with Mr Peter Gerrard as our leading surgeon in this field. We've had our share of famous visitors too. In 1985 Queen Elizabeth visited the children of Henton Hospital, and at Christmas last year the Prime Minister had lunch with the patients. And one of our best friends is comedian Johnny Brown whose family live in this area, and who has tirelessly raised thousands of pounds for hospital equipment including the new body scanner bought last month.

Thank you very much Johnny. Don't forget his next visit which is on Saturday evening in the community centre. And lastly, let's mention Radio Henton itself, which started in 1972, broadcasting just 2 hours a day. Now we're on the air from six in the morning to six at night. Well that's all from me for today. I hope you enjoyed the programme. Now back to Mike for some musical entertainment.

That is the end of Section 2. You now have half a minute to check your answers.

Skills Focus   Speaking - Intonation in questions

Listen to the five questions and decide if they sound polite or not.

1	Can I open the window?	*(polite)*
2	Where do you live?	*(not polite)*
3	Are you English?	*(not polite)*
4	Do you want some coffee?	*(polite)*
5	Do you mind if I smoke?	*(not polite)*

Now listen to six more questions and decide if the voice goes up or down. We have done the first one for you.

1	Are you married?	*(up)*
2	Do you like mangoes?	*(up)*
3	Where are you from?	*(down)*
4	How long have you been here?	*(down)*
5	Could you tell me your name, please?	*(up on 'please')*
6	Would you mind opening the window?	*(down)*

Unit 8   Listening

Section 1

Two students are talking about a diploma course. As you listen, decide if the different components of the diploma were interesting or not and how difficult they were. Put ticks in the corresponding columns of the table in your book. The first one has been done for you as an example. First stop the tape for half a minute and study the table.

Now listen carefully and put your ticks in the table.

Student A: Mark, you did the diploma last year didn't you?

Mark (M): Yeah, that's right. Yeah.

A: Because I, er, I'm thinking about doing it next year and well, do you mind if I ask you to tell me some things.

M: Not at all, no, of course.

A: I mean, I know it starts with an orientation course, doesn't it?

M: Yeah, it does. You do an orientation in London. The rest of it's, er, sent by post. Yeah, the orientation I felt, was a bit of a waste of time, really. Nothing very challenging. I felt I knew most of it really.

A:	How long was it?
M:	A couple of weeks.
A:	Er, I mean, I've got to do it have I?
M:	Yeah, I'm afraid it's compulsory.
A:	Oh right. And then what are the other parts, once you've got away from the orientation course what do you have to do?
M:	Well, there's a big written component. You do a lot of written work. Mainly essays and exercises. Um, which um, were OK, not easy, but not difficult really um, and challenging – I enjoyed writing a lot of the essays. About one every three weeks or so.
A:	So, you had to do a lot of reading for that, and things, which must have been quite good.
M:	Yeah.
A:	And then of course, there's the practical component I suppose.
M:	Yeah, yeah, every, I suppose, four or six weeks you're observed teaching a class.
A:	Ugh!
M:	Um, and again that's quite a challenge and because it's not an exam it was OK, I'd say, OK.
A:	Why was it OK, what do you mean, it was ...?
M:	Well, I mean it wasn't an examination. When it came to the actual practical exams, now they're hard. They really are. A lot of stress, not very enjoyable at all.
A:	Yes, they sound terrifying.
M:	And then of course, finally, there were written exams as well. Um, and a lot of people find those very difficult, but um, in my case I'm quite good at writing timed essays, so they were, I suppose, fair, they weren't too bad for me. Just rather dull, you know, sitting down and writing for six hours.
A:	Yes.

That is the end of Section 1. You now have half a minute to check your answers.

Now go to Section 2.

Section 2

A student is researching how schools in Britain have changed over the last ten years. He interviews Diana about her school days. As you listen, answer questions 5-13 by writing a word or short phrase in the space provided. First, stop the tape and study questions 5-13.

Now listen and answer questions 5-13.

Student A:	So Diana you went to a comprehensive school in London?
Diana (D):	No, no I didn't. I went to a grammar school.
A:	Oh, a grammar school, right I see. Can you remember what sort of size were the classes?
D:	Yes, I, er, remember very well. Forty in most of the classes.
A:	Uh-huh, right, I see. And, can you remember, before the exam years, in perhaps the first three years of school, what subjects were compulsory at your school?

D: Oh dear, well, oh dear. Um, English was compulsory, maths, um, geography, history, sport.

A: I see, quite a lot. And when it came to the exams how many 'O' levels were you able to take?

D: What do you mean? Me personally or everybody?

A: Anybody. I mean was there a maximum?

D: Well, I took eight, I think some people took nine, I don't think anybody took more than that in one year.

A: A more general question. How did you feel about discipline levels at school? Did you feel it was very strong, the discipline, firm?

D: Yes, yes, um, I remember certain teachers that we felt were unable to keep it and, of course, we took advantage of that, but basically I think it was rather well done. Not too overt really.

A: Hmm, was there any physical punishment?

D: No, no, not at all.

A: Yeah. Um, did you have to wear a uniform?

D: Yes.

A: In all years?

D: No, sixth form didn't have to. Um, but from years one to five it was compulsory.

A: What sort of uniform?

D: Er, a blue tunic, blouse and tie.

A: Right, um.

D: But actually they did change it sort of half way through. They allowed us to wear trousers in the winter. Because this was a girls' school remember.

A: Right, yeah, yeah, I see. And one final thing. Back in the first, say, three years of grammar school, how often did you have exams?

D: At the end of every term.

A: Uh-huh, so three times a year. OK, thanks very much.

D: Thank you.

That is the end of Section 2. You now have half a minute to check your answers.

Unit 9   Listening

Section 1

Two friends are discussing what's on this week in their town. As you listen to the recording fill in the gaps numbered 1-8 in the chart. First stop the tape for one minute and study the chart on page 116 in your book.

Now listen carefully and fill the gaps numbered 1-8.

A: Hey, Peter. Is that the local paper?

B: Yes, it's just come. Why?

A: Oh, I just wondered what's on this week. Are there any good films?

B: Films ... hold on, where's the entertainments page, do you know?

A: Near the back I think.

B: Got it. Oh, nothing very exciting, although on Tuesday there's a single showing of 'Time Off' at the Odeon which everybody says is really good.

A: Oh right. What time is it on?

B: Hmm. 9.30.

A: That's a pity, it's too late. I've got an early start the next morning. Any theatre?

B: That comedy's still running at the Palace.

A: Which one?

B: 'Chicken' – that's every day except Monday, 7.30, with a 2.30 matinee on Saturday. Are you interested?

A: Maybe, I don't know.

B: Oh, hang on, this looks interesting ... that man, Robert Smith, from the TV 'Nature' programme is coming to the Town Hall to give a talk.

A: Really? What about?

B: It's called 'The good, the bad and the ozone', guess what it's about!

A: Well, it's certainly very topical. Does it cost anything?

B: No, it's free.

A: Guess it has to be that then! When is it?

B: Wednesday at 7.00. I'll come too.

A: Sounds interesting.

That is the end of Section 1. Stop the tape for half a minute and check your answers.

Section 2

The two friends decide to go to the talk, given by Robert Smith, on the subject of the ozone layer. As you listen to the first part of the talk, answer questions 9-18 by writing a word or a short phrase in the space provided. The first one is done for you as an example. Now stop the tape for one minute and look at questions 9-18.

Speaker: Well, welcome to the town hall this evening – it's a pleasure to see so many faces. I'm going to talk, as you know, about one of the most controversial topics of the present day; about ozone, a gas which is vital to life on earth.

Ozone, spread thinly in the Earth's stratosphere, about 10 km to 50 km above ground level, is essential to all forms of life. The molecules of ozone at that level 'filter out' high energy ultraviolet (UV) radiation from the sun, and in doing so protect plants and animals from harmful UV rays. Many scientists believe that certain forms of life were unable to live on land before the ozone layer had formed.

But, nearer the ground, ozone is a problem, and by the sea it may even damage your health. Scientists now believe that the invigorating effect that comes from being near the sea is not caused by ozone in the atmosphere, but instead is a result of ions (electrically charged particles) in the sea air. Similarly, the distinctive smell of the sea probably comes from old fish and rotting seaweed, rather than ozone.

But even more serious than the effect of ozone by the sea is its high level of concentration in polluted cities all over the world.

In the past, London was so famous for its smogs that the city was commonly known as 'the Smoke'. These smogs were thick, smoky fogs which enveloped the city, and they persisted until the early 1960s. Coal-burning fires were the major cause of this health hazard, which was not eradicated until legislation was enacted in the late 1950s, setting up 'smokeless zones' and controlling the types of fuel that could be burned. But recently, a new type of smog has hit the headlines – of which one of the constituent parts is ozone. The combination of exhaust gases from cars and factories, still air, warmth and clear sunshine, has resulted in a highly poisonous form of ozone. Sunlight encourages a chemical reaction which changes oxygen in the air to ozone – hence the name 'photochemical smog'; even small amounts of ozone can irritate people's eyes, give them headaches and affect their breathing. Higher concentrations can also damage plant tissues, and may have other, more severe, consequences. In short, ozone is best kept at a distance from plants and animals.

So when does ozone become a friend to life on earth? Well ... the molecules of ozone ensure that a good deal of UV radiation is prevented from reaching people and plants on Earth (and within 10 km of the earth). This is good news for plants – because crops such as maize, wheat and rice give lower and poorer quality yields if too much UV radiation reaches them.
It is good news for human beings too – high levels of UV radiation can cause malignant melanomas, or skin cancers, some of which may be capable of spreading to other parts of the body if they are not treated at an early stage. Why is it that ozone has become so well-known in the last decade? The answer involves ozone itself, UV radiation, and a family of chemicals called chlorofluorocarbons (or CFCs).
CFCs were first demonstrated by the American inventor Thomas Midgley when he inhaled a lungful of CFC gas and used it to blow out a candle. This showed two vital properties of CFCs: they do not burn and they are not poisonous. For this reason they became the ideal replacement for ammonia in refrigerators: ammonia is toxic, inflammable, and has an unpleasant smell.
The CFC family of chemicals has many other uses, for example, inside aerosols. Within the can, the CFC is a liquid; when the pressure is released it becomes a gas. Other uses are as cleaning solvents.
In Thomas Midgley's time, CFCs seemed the answer to many problems. Unfortunately, each time they are used some of the gas escapes into the atmosphere. CFCs are very stable – it takes perhaps 75 years before they break down. They remain in the air and reach high into the atmosphere.
This is where the problems begin. Up in the stratosphere, conditions seem to be perfect for breaking down CFCs and releasing chlorine. This is especially true during the cold winters above the South Pole in Antarctica. In temperatures of below –80C, atoms of chlorine are formed. When the sun returns in spring, the chlorine becomes an ozone destroyer.
Just one chlorine atom can destroy thousands of ozone molecules.

Now listen carefully and answer questions 9-18.

That is the end of Section 2. Stop the tape for half a minute and check your answers.

Section 3

As you listen to the next part of the talk, fill in the gaps numbered 19-25 by writing in the missing words in the column to the right of the passage. Stop the tape for one minute and study questions 19-25.

Now listen carefully and answer questions 19-25.

Speaker: The scientist Joe Farman, until recently head of the British Antarctic Survey team which has been carrying out research in the Antarctic for the past 20 years, first reported the 'hole' above Antarctica in 1985. Experts think that the hole is as big in area as the United States (approximately 9 500 000 sq km) and as deep as the height of Mount Everest (nearly 8850 m). Every southern summer – early in November – the Antarctic hole breaks up into blobs of ozone-reduced air that drift around in the southern hemisphere. In December 1987 one of these blobs drifted over parts of Australia and New Zealand. Above Melbourne, where three million people live, it was reported that the ozone levels fell by more than 10 per cent for about three days. The effects of such depletion are not known; possible consequences could include a significant rise in the number of malignant melanomas. Eventually the concentration of ozone in the stratosphere could be diluted over a large area of the Earth. Again, it is likely that deaths from malignant melanoma will result. Why do governments not just ban CFCs? The United States banned their use in aerosols three years ago, since when few countries have followed.

Manufacturers have been working to find a replacement for CFCs which will not damage the ozone layer, and which does not have other harmful properties. Butane and propane have been suggested for use in refrigerators, but both of these are a fire risk, because they burn easily. It is thought that if propane in a refrigerator leaked near a pilot light it could explode, but it is also argued that the tubes containing the propane could be safely sealed.

Some scientists believe that we should not have been so quick to condemn CFCs. They argue that gases from burning vegetation and wood-rotting fungi do far more damage to the ozone layer.

Even so, the effect of CFCs as a 'greenhouse' gas in warming the Earth is significant. The search to replace CFCs continues. But it is hoped that any replacement will not have the unforeseen side effects of Thomas Midgley's discovery in 1930.

Skills Focus   Speaking - Speculating about the future

Listen to the dialogue and answer the two questions.

A: What do you think about this statement – 'My children will inherit the consequences of our abuse of the earth's resources.'?

B: Hmm. Well I think it's probably true.

A: Why?

B: Well, I think that it's our generation that's seen a huge rise in the use of fossil fuels. We're using up the forests of the world, we're using up the coal, well think of the consumption of oil. It's absolutely colossal!

A: Yeah. But this is talking about the consequences in the future. I mean what consequences?

B: Well, I suppose it's going to run out, isn't it. I mean there won't be any oil. Perhaps our children will still have it, but looking further ahead our grandchildren, great-grandchildren, those generations are just not going to have oil, coal, gas, to use.

A: And what about things like global warming? Do you believe what scientists say?

B: Umm. Well, I think it's still uncertain, but it's certainly another example of abuse. I think it's a very serious problem that because we burn so much coal and oil we're destroying the ozone layer. I mean, I suppose it's true to say that our children will inherit the consequences of our abuse but I think they will also inherit the awareness that has come from that abuse. There's an awful lot of knowledge now about how we're destroying the atmosphere and the environment even if we continue to do it. But perhaps at least that knowledge will enable people to do something about it in future generations.

Unit 10   Listening

Section 1

Janet and Paul are talking about a university competition in which Paul is taking part. As you listen you will have to choose the best alternative, **A, B, C** or **D**, and circle the letter. The first one has been done for you as an example. First, stop the tape for one minute and study questions 1-6.

Now, listen carefully, and answer questions 1-6.

Janet (J):   I've seen the posters for the Mastermind Quiz tonight, um, is that the same as that television programme 'Mastermind'? I mean, what kind of competition is it exactly?

Paul (P):   Oh, it's not quite the same as the television one, they have specific topics, don't they ...? No, this one, um, it's a general knowledge quiz, though we can choose categories, you know, we can answer on sport, or history, or literature, so we can choose in each question.

J: So are you actually on your own, like, you know, you sit in a big black chair like on the television?

P: No, no, there are four of us, four in a team.

J: Oh, how did you find team-mates, I mean is it sort of chosen by subject, or ...

P: Oh, no, no, nobody chose, we, um we just really got together one evening, heard about it, thought it'd be a good idea to make a team – it was nothing very carefully planned.

J: So how come you're in the final then – have you had to go through lots of rounds?

P: Well, this is the fourth time we've had to do it. It's been going all term actually. It's been a couple of weeks between each round but, er, but we were a bit lucky actually, I mean we won the first two rounds that we were in, um, then in the third one another team was accused of cheating, so um, we actually got through rather luckily, we thought we were second, but er, we got through.

J: How did they cheat? What, what did they do?

P: Oh, I think they'd managed to get some of the questions the day before, and they'd photocopied them, and er, learnt the answers with the help of an encyclopaedia.

J: Oh, great! Well, I think I'd quite like to come and see it actually ... Where is it? I didn't read the poster very carefully, I'm afraid.

P: Oh, it's over in the um, the medical building, um, and it's on the ground floor, um, in the old lecture room, you know, just past Laboratory 2, do you know that one?

J: Um, I think I could probably find it. What time does it start?

P: Well, it's supposed to start at about 8, but it'll probably be a few minutes later than that, I suspect, um, and probably be over by about half past nine I should think, and er, I hope, if we win, um, we'll be having a party after that.

J: Um, should I get tickets, and if so, where can I get them?

P: Um, well, you can buy them in the university shop, but they're probably sold out by now. I don't think you need to, I would just get them on the door if I were you, turn up just before 8, buy them on the door.

J: OK, I'm gonna go. Right, well, best of luck!

P: Thanks a lot. See you later.

J: I'll be rooting for you!

That is the end of Section 1. Stop the tape for half a minute, and check your answers.

Now go to Section 2.

Section 2

Following a number of thefts and break-ins at the university, a policeman comes to give the students safety and security advice. As you listen, fill in the gaps numbered 7-16 in the notes with one or two words. First, stop the tape for one minute and study the notes.

Now listen, and fill in the gaps numbered 7-16.

Policeman: Well, hello everybody, um, thank you very much for inviting me here, um, and it's very pleasant to have a chance to talk to you about some things which are obviously very much on everybody's minds. I want to talk about three areas of security, safety: firstly bicycles, I know a lot of you have bikes, secondly housing, whether private or college housing and finally I'll mention a word or two about personal security.

So firstly, bikes. When you get your bike, whether it's new or second-hand, bring it as soon as possible to the police station. There we'll be able to stamp it with a serial number, we actually stamp it into the metal, um, we'll register the number, put it on our list, OK, this is er, a great er, deterrent to criminals if they realise there's a number stamped on it. Make sure you buy a good lock, um, it *can* be expensive, but it's *never* a waste of money. Um, if you have an expensive bike it's worth buying two locks, if you have quick-release wheels you can fit one lock at the front and one at the back. Do spend money on a good lock, um, the cheap locks can be very, very easy to cut. Um, make sure you lock the bike to something permanent, though do be considerate to pedestrians. And if the worst happens, you lose your bike, immediately report it to us, quoting that serial number that you should have had stamped.

OK um, housing. Well, if you're in college accommodation, a few points to bear in mind: er, you'll notice the doors of your college rooms have two types of lock, a Yale lock and a Chubb lock – make sure you *double*-lock your door, not just one lock, both of them, however long you're going out for. Some people go out for a short time, and they think they don't need to double-lock the door; you should *always* double-lock the door. Make sure when you go out all the windows are closed, um, those of you on the ground and first floor college rooms will notice that you've got locking windows – make sure you use them. Lock them every time you go out, lock them at night. If you've got expensive equipment in your college room, belonging to you or the college, first of all insure it. So many people lose things and haven't got insurance – make sure you insure it, and make sure that you register it either with the college or with the police. Again for a small fee we can actually stamp the serial number on to most types of equipment.

For those of you in private accommodation, um, again make sure there's a good lock on the front door, make sure you know who exactly has a key to the door – how many people? Again, check the windows close properly, make sure you leave them closed whenever you go out, and put a safety chain on the door. That means you can open the door a couple of inches, find out who it is at the door, um, and of course let them in if you know who they are, or stop them from coming in if you don't know who they are.

That brings me on to *personal* security. Er, I think it hardly needs saying, wherever possible, avoid walking alone late at night, especially women. Avoid dark streets, a lot of streets in this town are very badly lit, try and stick to the well-lit streets whenever possible. Carry something noisy with you – a whistle is an excellent idea, a whistle is cheap, it can make a lot of noise very quickly, um, in any kind of emergencies. Carry a whistle with you. Also if you know you're going to be out late, make sure you've got enough money for a taxi to get home again, or arrange to stay with friends closer to where you'll be during the evening. It may sound absurd but don't forget, the university actually offers free self-defence classes. I hope it's something you'd never have to use, but, um, it's certainly worth going along to a few self-defence sessions.
All this sounds a little bit extreme, um, I think perhaps the way to sum it up is to say that sensible precautions could prevent serious problems, um, I think a few small steps prevent much worse things happening. OK, are there any questions at this stage ...?

That is the end of Section 2. Stop the tape for half a minute and check your answers.

Now go to Section 3

Section 3

Janet decides it's time to learn how to use a computer, and goes to the computer room in her college. She asks someone there how to use the computer. As you listen, decide if statements 17-25 are true, false, or if the information is not given, and write T, F or NG in the boxes provided. First, stop the tape for one minute, and study statements 17-25.

Now listen, and answer questions 17-25.

Janet (J):	Er, excuse me, can you help me?
Other student (OS):	Oh, yeah, sure. What's the problem?
J:	Well, I've never used a computer before I'm afraid, so I have very little idea what to do.
OS:	Oh, yeah, OK, sure, well you'd better start at the beginning then ... Well first you need to switch it on.
J:	Well, how do I do that?

OS: Right, well there are two switches, one of them's on the monitor, the TV screen, that's on the side there, got it? (yeah) OK, switch that one on, OK, and um, the other switch is on the main unit, in the middle here, this box, so just switch that one on (right), OK. Now we've just got to wait for a minute or so while the computer checks itself out, um, so you hold on, you can see various figures on the screen ... now just wait until, right, here it is, you see this coloured thing, this is the *menu*.

J: What does that mean exactly?

OS: The menu is just the list of programs which are on the computer so you can choose the one, the one you want.

J: Well, I just want to do some typing, type my essay, so what do I want actually?

OS: Right, you want the word processor, you can see it there, right, you see the arrow key, down on the right, (yeah) OK, just keep pressing the down arrow until the black line appears on the word processor (right, OK), that's it, OK, and now press 'enter' to select ... (where's that?)... on the right, just above the arrows, right (press it?) right, OK, so now you can see that, there we are, there's the title, 'Word processor', um, just wait a few seconds longer, there we are, blank screen, you could just start typing now, as if it's a typewriter.

J: Er, OK ... what about if I make a mistake, I know it'll correct it, how do I do that?

OS: OK, um, well, the arrow keys you used before, you can use those to move back through what you've typed, and um, when you get the, er, see the little flashing line, the *cursor*, when that's under your mistake, just press 'delete', and type in whatever you want to correct it to. Very important is saving your document (what do you mean?). Well, er, putting it in the computer's memory, so that you can go away, come back to it, and, er, you see this list of words above the keyboard (yes) you see just above the button called F10, there's a word, 'save' (right). So to save your document press that F10, OK, now you can see it asks you for a name, so now you need to type in a name you want to call your document.

J: Does that have, are there any, er, rules about that, how many letters can it have?

OS: Um, I think it's up to 8 letters.

J: OK, so if I call it by my name, Janet?

OS: Right, OK, and press 'enter' again, and there you can see it's, er, it's saving it for you. Next time you do that, you're half way through a document, just press F10, and it will um, flash up the name 'Janet' for you and you can just press 'enter'.

J: OK, er, it seems quite easy actually, but now the thing that I have no idea how to do is print it out.

OS: Right, OK, well the printer's connected, just make sure the printer is switched on, at the bottom, the black switch, then you move the cursor to where you can see it written on the list, print. You need to press two buttons, one is the shift key, got that?

J: Er, no, where is that?

OS: On the left, like for upper case letters.

J: Oh right. OK.

OS: And then F7, at the top.

J: OK.

OS: Right. And now you can see it says on the screen 'Print document?' with a question mark, and we just say 'yes'.

J: So do I have to type 'YES' – Y - E - S?

OS: No just press 'Y'.

J: Oh right, yeah.

OS: And there's paper feeding permanently into the printer, so we just press 'Y' and it will print it for you, but for now let's just cancel it. The other thing you need to know is, um, how to finish, er, how to exit. I'll tell you what – I'll go and get on with my work and er, let me know when you've finished, and I'll come and help you exit.

J: Oh thanks very much, you've been very helpful and kind. Thank you. Will you be here actually?

OS: Yeah I'm going to be here for the next couple of hours, so, er, sure.

J: So if I get stuck you can help me?

OS: Yep, of course.

J: Thanks a lot.

That is the end of Section 3. Stop the tape for half a minute and check your answers.

Now go to Section 4.

Section 4

Before starting her course, Janet spent a year travelling abroad. Paul is talking to her about her travels. As you listen to their conversation, answer questions 26-33 by writing a word or short phrase in the space provided. First stop the tape for one minute and study questions 26-33.

Now listen carefully and answer questions 26-33.

J: Well, it seems quite common actually. Lots of people in Australia now are travelling and taking time off. And when I was actually travelling I met so many people doing the same thing.

P: Yeah, yeah, so where did you start off?

J: Well, I went to New Zealand first, um, and got a job in an insurance company as a secretary. And I worked there for three months.

P: Really? You can do that, can you? I mean, it's possible for somebody to get work in New Zealand without being a New Zealander?

J: Australians and New Zealanders can exchange either – you know you can work in either country.

P: Right, yeah.

J: So that was easy. So I worked there for three months and raised the money for the rest of the travels really. So from there I went to Indonesia and travelled around the different islands of Indonesia, Malaysia, Singapore, Thailand, China, Nepal and India.

P: What about in Indonesia, what did you do, did you fly mostly between the islands?

J: Er, I did a bit of that and boats, local boats.

P: And what about, er, Singapore? People say it's very very modern but because it's so modern it's rather boring. Did you find that?

J: Um, it's difficult to say. It has different attractions. It's a great big shopping centre basically, and I really enjoyed it from that point of view, and, um, it was very clean. It's true there isn't a lot of history there now, er, they've wiped a lot of it out. But I did enjoy it. I think it's worth a visit.

P: And after, you said you went what, to Singapore, Malaysia, Thailand, and then China? That's quite a hard country to travel in, isn't it?

J: Er, it was quite hard, yeah. But it was fabulous, it really was. You haven't been there then?

P: No I haven't, no. I mean it's very big, isn't it – did you ...?

J: Yeah, well I only had two months travelling in China and that was too short. I felt I didn't have enough time, so I sacrificed a lot of places and did the main tourist routes really. But I was lucky enough to get into Tibet before it was closed to tourists, and that was brilliant.

P: Yeah. What was the most interesting place you visited, do you think?

J: Well I think actually Tibet was the most fascinating and exciting – I've never been anywhere so different. The people are wonderful – the clothes they wear, the food they eat.

P: And you said you went to Nepal as well.

J: Yes, um, that was sort of an easier version of Tibet really, and there are a lot of Tibetans there as well as other tribes and Nepalis. So that was good because I went trekking in Nepal. You should do that.

P: How long did you trek for?

J: Oh, I only did a short one, only for a week, I was lazy.

P: Was it very exhausting?

J: No, it wasn't actually. I mean you just set your own pace and don't push yourself – that would be stupid. Um, you don't have to walk very far. Er, so that was great.

P: So how did it feel after all this travelling – how did it feel to stop travelling? I mean you were on the move for months and months and suddenly you're here and, er, not travelling any more. How does it feel?

J: Oh, I was ready to stop. You get pretty sick of wearing the same clothes and washing them in different hotels, and never staying in the same place for longer than two days and things. I was ready to stop. I don't think I could keep doing it. I mean I've met people who've been travelling for two, three years – I couldn't do it.

P: Yeah, yeah. Well maybe it's something I should try after this.

J: Oh, I think you should.

That is the end of Section 4. Stop the tape for half a minute and check your answers.

It is nearly the end of this listening test. You now have a further one minute to look over all your answers and then your teacher will tell you to stop writing.